des | Rowan's | Shannahan & Wrightson | Fox's formerly Dawson's | Fox's | Rexall formerly Apothecary Shop | Adkinson's formerly Thompson & Kersey | Rileys | Dover Road

UARE, EASTON, MARYLAND

LE EVIDENCE, BY HENRY CHANDLEE FORMAN, A.I.A., ARCHITECT

Tidewater Maryland Architecture

and

Gardens

TIDEWATER MARYLAND

ARCHITECTURE

AND

GARDENS

A SEQUEL TO

Early Manor and Plantation Houses of Maryland

BY

HENRY CHANDLEE FORMAN

P.H.D. (FINE ARTS), A.I.A.

ARCHITECTURAL BOOK PUBLISHING COMPANY, INC.

NEW YORK

To

James W. Foster

and

The Maryland Historical Society

ACKNOWLEDGMENTS

The following persons or organizations graciously loaned or gave photographs:

Mr. John H. Scarff
Mrs. Maynard Vilas Barney
Mr. James C. Wilfong, Jr.
Miss Frances Benjamin Johnston
Mr. H. Robins Hollyday
Mr. Edward H. Hammond
Mrs. C. M. Robinson
Mrs. J. Spence Howard
Mrs. M. C. Oxenham
Mrs. Ethan Allen Carey
Mrs. Edward Lee Carey
Mr. C. Lowndes Johnson
The Historic American Buildings Survey
The Collections of the Library of Congress

These persons or organizations kindly assisted with some of the textual material, in one manner or another:

Mr. and Mrs. W. H. Bosley
Mrs. A. L. Ferguson
Mrs. F. H. Schofield
Mr. and Mrs. Miodrag Blagojevich
Miss Anne Corse
Mrs. Alan Leroy Carter
Miss Mary Corse
Mr. Fred Shelley
Lt. C. A. Kirtley, U.S.N.,Ret.
Mr. Edward H. Hammond
Mr. William D. Pitts
Mr. and Mrs. Morgan Schiller
Mrs. Gordon Fisher, Jr.
Mrs. Margaret Dickson
Mrs. Anna E. Harper
Col. Harrison Tilghman
Mr. and Mrs. G. A. Van Lennap
Lt. Comdr. Julian H. Maynard, U.S.N.
Dr. Guy Steele
Mrs. Arthur P. Sewell
Mr. Townsend Scott, Jr.
Maryland Historical Magazine
The Star-Spangled Banner Flag House Association

CONTENTS

CONTENTS

INTRODUCTION

ONCE more we take up the pen, to jot down these ideas about Maryland, to make all the drawings, and to take most of the photographs of this work. By choice we have designated this study the sequel, or volume two, of *Early Manor and Plantation Houses of Maryland* (1934), a compendium of old homes, still in print.

It is hoped that this work will form part of a three-volume set on Maryland. Its purpose is to make a record of civilization by preserving on paper, for always, buildings of the following categories: those which have been completely destroyed, are in the last stages of disintegration, have been hopelessly changed by what we designated in 1934 as "so-called improvements," or may suffer such fates in the future.

The objective of *Early Manors* is the same as this book, namely, to "take up the challenge to gather and preserve this ancient and priceless material before it is forever lost. Priceless, because the principles of good building, as shown herein, will last always."

Apropos of preservation, the society founded for the purpose usually "preserves" for posterity two or three distinguished buildings. But when four or five hundred structures built before 1800 in Maryland are each year destroyed or hopelessly changed in character by "improvements" which are "no better than fire," then it is time that something more should be done. The present work has been written accepting the challenge to record some of these edifices before it is too late.

This writer may "make good at a ruinous occupation," [1] by restoring dilapidated structures and tumbled-down ruins to their former condition and beauty. But there is no one, we sincerely believe, who realizes how fast these old buildings in the Free State become lost to us: one spark, or one building contractor, and they are gone or changed.

This is not an architectural history, like the writer's work, *The Architecture of the Old South* (1948), which treats of the history of the Medieval Style in the Southern Colonies, based upon the comparative method. On the contrary, this book is intended to be a series of concise monographs of Maryland gardens and buildings, classified regionally, for the purposes of making a record and of showing the beauty of a time and place which have changed.

In many instances there is related something of the field work involved—the hard labor, obstacles, disappointments, and even injuries. *This* is no armchair work. How many afternoons or evenings have we returned home exhausted, from an old ruin or a new discovery. Long after we are placed beneath a Quaker tombstone, this work will be of value to those who appreciate the past in order to understand the present. It will be said that *he* was an historian, *he* recorded and interpreted the past. And the facts that he spent eleven years studying the arts in universities and in foreign galleries and museums, and that he held for years top professional rank in American colleges, teaching fine arts and archaeology, will not be remembered.

Looking through these pages, the reader will probably notice that in the floor plans some of the names of the rooms are different from those used today. In early Maryland the living room was called "the Hall," "the Great Hall," or "the Great Room." "The Hall" was never a passageway. At *Resurrection Manor* in Maryland, for example, "the Hall" in 1664 contained one couch, three small tables, four leather chairs, and the like.

Immediately above "the Hall" lay "the Hall Chamber," because it was the custom to designate the space over a particular room by the word "chamber." Thus, at *Compton*, Talbot County, the room above "the Hall" was "the Chamber over the Hall." In the same manner, the area over "the Parlor," which generally adjoined "the Hall," was "the Parlor Chamber." Following suit, "the Porch Chamber," was the little room over the enclosed porch.

The attic was usually spoken of as "the Garret," or "the Loft." Nevertheless, when the word, "supra-attic," is met with in the text, this writer must admit his coinage. Sometimes in early times it was necessary to be more specific in describ-

[1] Article by Miss Katherine Scarborough, *Baltimore Sun*, June 20, 1954.

ing a room, as, for instance, "the Chamber over the New Room," or "the Chamber on the right hand above Staires." A guest or rented room was called "the Lodging Chamber."

"The Kitchen," or "Kitching," as it was occasionally pronounced, had above it "the Kitchen Chamber," over which, in its turn, lay the little cramped space known as "the Kitchen Loft." Next to "the Kitchen" was very often "the Kitchen Buttery." And thereby hangs a tale. In one New England dwelling administered by a preservation society "the buttery" is today furnished with wooden receptacles and accessories for holding and making butter. Unfortunately for romance, "the buttery" was not named for butter, but for bottles. In large houses and mansions the bottlery, or *boterie*, was presided over by the butler or bottle-bearer—the *bouteillier*. All of which is apropos of our Maryland "buttery," progenitor of the pantry.

When the kitchen stood off to itself, it was known as "the Kitchen House."

The basement was "the Cellar"; and in at least one dwelling in the Free State there was a "Cellar Loft." The reader is left to puzzle out that one.

Very often in the early days the stairway was referred to as "the payre of stayres." The compartment in which the stairs rose to an upper floor was called "the Case," or "the Stair Case." In the great brick State House of 1676 in St. Mary's City, the first capital of Maryland, the tower at the rear was known as "the Stair Case." Again, when the stairs were boarded in, box-like, they comprised "the stairs sealed"; but when open, and when they rose around the sides of a room, they were called "open well" stairs—an arrangement considered by the British as a waster of space.

The farm was "the plantation," meaning the place for planting. When the owner's home was situated on such a spot, it was called "the dwelling plantation," or sometimes "the home plantation."

Much as it may surprise some readers, a plantation in Maryland was not necessarily a "manor." The Lord Proprietary of the Province granted manors with certain accompanying privileges. First, a manor comprised usually a large tract of a thousand or more acres. Second, courts leet and courts baron were held upon the manor land. Make no mistake about it; without your own law courts functioning on your property, you had no manor. Many a building standing today in the Free State has no right to the appellation, "manor."

The wharf on Chesapeake Bay or tidal tributary from which you had your tobacco or other staples shipped directly to England, and upon which your wife and daughter received their bundles of silks, satins, and damask, was called "the Landing." Around the plantation dwelling or the manor house were usually numerous subsidiary buildings called "outhouses," sometimes forming a small village.

When an outbuilding was an integral and necessary part of a composition in which the main building or residence formed the center, it is today called a "dependency." Some recent writers have been claiming that any outhouse is a dependency, but they are wrong. The test is simple: if the removal of the outbuilding makes a gaping hole in the composition, then the structure is a dependency.

The names of the outhouses are legion, and mention of a few will suffice. In the old days the dairy was called "the Milk House," and its upper floor when it had one, "the Milk House Chamber." The slave or servant's building was "the Quarters." Such cabins and cottages were usually of the most primitive sort, yet far better than the circular mud or wooden huts in Central Africa from which the Negroes came. In early Maryland the blacks were considered the property of the master, and in the estate inventories were listed along with the cattle, as at the *Resurrection Manor* (1664). In a Queen Anne's County inventory of 1773, the quarters were referred to as "the Negro House."

The corn crib was known as the "Corn House," the chicken house as "the Hen House," and the carriage shed as "the Chaise House." The smoke house was sometimes called "the Meat House."

Throughout the text we have referred often to "the outshut." That is the old English name for shed or "wart," the small projecting addition to a building. Now the word outshut may not have been employed in the vocabulary of early Maryland, but it is an expressive and authentic term. In that connection, "the chimney pent," the little closet with a one-slope roof next to an outside chimney, may be classified as an outshut.

When we consider the parts of an early building, we find that some terms are not exactly as we today know them. A dormer was a "dormant," or "lutarn window." When a roof was hipped, it was called an "Italian," or "pyramid," roof. Steeples were "pyramids," too, as in *St. Andrew's Church*, St. Mary's County, herein described. The gable end was termed "the gavil end," and the fireplace was called "the chimney," or "the chimney piece." In specifying a fireplace for each room of an edifice, the early builders would state that "to each room was to be a chimney of brick." If they possessed a beamed fireplace, it might be called a "white oak mantel tree."

The room features had their own vernacular. The "summer" was the great beam or girder which usually crossed the middle of a room, and "joists" were the small beams. In one dwelling of 1659 there were, it is recorded, "a summer and small joists." In the text we have incorporated two modern descriptive terms: the "lie-on-your-stomach" window and the "knock-head." In a literal sense the first refers to a small window in the gable near the floor level, but in a broad meaning, it is any small window in a gable whether near the floor or not. The knock-head is descriptive of bedchambers and lofts with sloping ceilings. In several lectures this writer has taken a knock at knock-heads, in spite of the fact that such rooms, used about eight or nine hours a day out of the twenty-four, are economical as far as building costs are concerned.

In the seventeenth century the standard window was the wood or iron casement on hinges. But by 1682, the date of the erection of the Third Haven Meetinghouse, Talbot County, the "sash," a sliding window, was just coming into fashion. Because these windows had no weights and pulleys, they are sometimes spoken of as "guillotine" windows. But casements were not abandoned all at once in Maryland; they hung on in isolated spots through the early eighteenth century.

The batten door was called the "plank door," because it was made up of boards, without panels. A "bolectioned door" was one having panels and raised mouldings around the panels.

When we come to the early outdoor "living rooms" of early Maryland, we find that such gardens were generally laid out on an axis between the main house and the water. "Falles" was the name given to grass terraces, and "forthrights" were the straight walks through the garden. Usually laid out in geometric fashion, the parterres were for the most part lined with small Dutch boxwood, above which flowers appeared. When we see in Free State gardens giant old boxwood bushes, we should realize that in size such bushes have far outstripped the original flowers.

Sometimes the parterres were filled with box instead of flowers; then the design became a knot pattern or a labyrinth, as may be seen in the drawings of *Perry Hall* and *El Don*.

An interesting garden design is that at *Burley Manor* in Worcester County, which demonstrates romantic and naturalistic tendencies of the early nineteenth century.

At least six architectural styles are referred to in the text, and an elementary knowledge of them is essential to an understanding of this work. Although outside the scope of this study, it should not be forgotten that the earliest style, *American Indian* architecture, flourished in the area which is now Maryland long before the white men came, and for many a year after they arrived there. The first whites were Virginians who formed temporary settlements (1622, 1624, 1628) within the limits of the Free State, and they introduced English architecture. But the real starting point for the English styles lies in the middle of certain tobacco fields in the first capital of Maryland, St. Mary's City.

Of the six architectural styles which prevailed in early Maryland, the writer has since 1934 discovered, identified, and named five of them. The Georgian Style was previously known.

The second, or *Medieval Style*, flourished from the founding of St. Mary's City in 1634 until the end of the seventeenth century. It was part and parcel of the Medieval Style of Great Britain. Among other features it is marked by steeply-pitched gables, separate chimney stacks, overhanging storeys, leaded-glass casements, exposed post-and-beam construction, and vertical-board paneling (p. 56).

The third, or *Jacobean Style*, which was widespread in England at the time of James I and afterward, in Maryland was a minor expression, grafted upon and dominated by the Medieval Style of the seventeenth century. It is chiefly characterized by curvilinear features, such as cupid's bows upon the heads of doors or windows, and on balusters and gables (p. 45, bottom).

In this book a good many examples belong to the fourth, or *Transitional Style*, which is a little more complicated than either the Medieval or the Jacobean, because it ran the gamut of experiments. By and large the Transitional Style forms the important connecting link between the Medieval Style of the seventeenth century and the Georgian of the eighteenth. Consequently, its dates overlap both centuries, and for our purposes, extend from about 1680 to around 1730. The style is generally marked by the introduction of the sash, or guillotine, window, already described.

The typical Transitional dwelling has little rooms added to the rear of the one-room-deep medieval building, one storey and loft high. In Britain these back rooms were called "cells," or "aisles," and in this work they are identified as such.

The writer has worked out a development classification for the "cell" building which is really very simple.[2] First came the "Early Cell" type of dwelling, where the gables are assymetrical and, at the rear, the "catslide" roof sweeps low to the ground (p. 143, bottom). The "Late Cell" type has symmetrical gables (p. 113). Although not as picturesque as the Early Cell type, it offers a more balanced and shipshape appearance.

The Transitional building also took other forms, such as the house with the gambrel roof (p. 145), or the narrow, one-room-deep home, its tall, slender gables rising two full storeys and garret high (p. 8).

The fifth, or *Georgian Style*, was prevalent in Maryland from about 1720 to around 1790, and came from England along with china, tea, and good manners. Marked by symmetry, balance, and formality, the style has a larger scale than the Medieval: higher ceilings, larger windows, and the like (p. 181). Its academic and pseudoclassic details include pediments, pilasters, engaged columns, quoins or corner blocks, and Palladian windows.

When in Maryland the Medieval, Jacobean, Transitional, and Georgian Styles

[2] See *The Architecture of the Old South*, pp. 86, 162; *Maryland Historical Magazine*, December, 1949, p. 275.

are met with beyond the periods when they flourished, they may be spoken of as forming a sixth style, the *Hangover*. For example a building in the medieval tradition dating from 1750, or even 1850, is *Hangover Medieval* (p. 90, bottom). It represents the "persistence of the Medieval Style" into a succeeding century. In the same way, a structure erected after 1730 in the Transitional manner is *Hangover Transitional* (p. 42).

Again, *Hangover Georgian*, a part of the great Federal or Early Republican Style of architecture, which commenced about 1785 or 1790, has been commonly but erroneously called Post Colonial. The Town Square Restoration of Easton on the Eastern Shore of Maryland, shown on the *endpapers*, is done not in Colonial or Post Colonial, but in Hangover Georgian.

Literally there is no such thing in the architecture of Tidewater Maryland as the Colonial Style or the Colonial Type—Eastern Shoremen, please note. The Colonial is a myth and has never existed at all. During the colonial period there were only the English styles, all of which have been briefly described.

In conclusion, it should be observed that in this volume the text and illustrations are copyrighted under the laws of the United States of America, and that no one may, in any fashion or manner, copy, borrow, or use the material in this book without written permission from the author and the publisher.

H. C. F.

Easton, Maryland

*The Great Room mantel at
Snow Hill Manor.*

1

THE LOWER EASTERN SHORE

1. *GENESAR* ON THE ATLANTIC OCEAN[1]

THE unfortunate and deplorable, but in many ways inevitable, destruction of the greater part of the remnants of colonial Maryland during the last century and a half may well be summed up today in that great brick pile, *Genesar*, green and gray in color, still lifting its proud but tottering head above the Atlantic Ocean beaches in Worcester County.

With the gradual ruin and continuous pillaging of *Genesar*, Maryland loses the most interesting building of the Transitional Style of architecture on the Eastern Shore if not in the entire State. Maryland becomes shorn of the best example, if not the only example, of Transitional paneling. And Maryland lets slip the richest glazed-brick patterns, or black diapering, in the whole State, and probably in the United States.

In the icy winter of 1932, this writer discovered *Genesar* at the end of a roadway several miles long, which was so muddy that it was almost impassable. From that visit the first published photograph (p. 34) of the mansion appeared in 1934.[2] In those days the house was empty, and all the handsome hand-carved woodwork remained except the stair balustrade. *Balusters gone* is the way it was expressed at that time in the field notes made at the site.

[1] This account was printed, with changes, in the *Maryland Historical Magazine*, March 1955.
[2] Forman, H. C., *Early Manor and Plantation Houses of Maryland*, Easton, Md., 1934, p. 141.

The history of *Genesar* goes back two hundred and seventy-nine years and connects several prominent families of the Eastern Shore. The land known as *Genesar* (the original name; also Genzar, Genessar, Genezir, Genezer) was patented on May 10, 1676, to the Honorable Colonel William Stevens, and comprised 2200 acres, "lying on the Sea Board side in Boquetonorton (Poqadenorton) Hundred on the south end of Sinepuxent Neck." Colonel Stevens, it appears, was one of the most important men of the Eastern Shore, a large property owner, and one of his Lordship's deputies for Maryland. He lived at *Rehobeth* on the Pocomoke River and in 1688 died there.

Nevertheless, Stevens did not long possess *Genesar*, for he assigned it to Edward Whale or Whaley and to Charles Ratcliffe, who received a patent for the whole 2200 acres on the 10th of January, 1679. Edward Whaley, who died in 1718, married Elizabeth Ratcliffe, a sister of Charles Ratcliffe. The tradition that this Edward Whaley was the "Regicide" at the time of King Charles I has been disproven by competent scholars.

The property was soon split into portions as follows: Charles Ratcliffe received 600 acres, Elian Ratcliffe 500, Nathaniel Ratcliffe of *Accomack* 300, and Edward Whaley 800. In 1709, upon the death of Charles Ratcliffe, his daughter Eliza received by will 200 acres of *Genesar*, his brother John Ratcliffe 100 acres, and his wife the remainder.

The existing mansion, *Genesar*, now popularly known as *Genezir*, is believed to have been constructed in 1732 by Major John Purnell, who died in 1756. The date of building is said to have been found among old manuscripts by a competent authority, but this writer has not been able to check it. At any rate, as far as the architecture of *Genesar* is concerned, the year 1732, which marks approximately the terminus of the Transitional Style, is satisfactory.[3] No date has been found on the structure itself.

Major John Purnell married Elizabeth Ratcliffe, and their sixth child, Thomas Purnell, who married a woman of his own family of Purnell, apparently lived at *Genesar*. During the American Revolutionary War the house is believed to have been occupied by either the above Thomas Purnell or his son Zadok Purnell.

In the early 1800s the property came into the possession of U. S. Senator John Selby Spence by his marriage with Maria, only daughter of Zadok Purnell. Senator Spence was born February 29, 1788, died October 22, 1840, and is buried in St. Paul's Churchyard, Berlin, Maryland. About 1867, approximately 700 acres along with the mansion were purchased by Zadok Purnell Henry I, from whom the place descended through his son of the same name to three heirs, John D.

[3] Forman, H. C., "The Transition in Maryland Architecture," *Maryland Historical Magazine*, December 1949, plate 1, p. 276.

Henry, Addie Byrd Henry (Mrs. Ethan Allen Carey), and Dr. Zadok Purnell Henry III, the last two of whom are still living. In 1939, *Genesar* was sold out of the Henry family.

Perhaps the moss-eaten brick pile has no claim to fame such as the event, "George Washington slept here," but there is a belief in the neighborhood that a ship of the British Navy during the War of 1812 fired upon *Genesar*. We know today that little harm came to the dwelling through cannon balls. The Maryland WPA *Guide* states that there may be bullet holes in the walls; "may" is a good word when one is not sure of his facts. Besides, *Genesar* was out of range of any ship of that time which lay off shore there.

But another tradition which may have more truth than fiction still persists through several generations of the Henry family. This is the story: during the American Revolution a British ship came through the North Beach inlet which no longer exists, and the owner of *Genesar*, at that time, Thomas (or Zadok) Purnell, became alarmed. He feared a landing party. The day was frigid, and the snow lay upon the ground. He armed his slaves with corn stocks and marched them in formation across the field in front of the house down to the shore, and then along the shore from one clump of trees to another. Then he had his slaves furtively crawl back to the house, form and march again over the same terrain. By this means he allowed time for his family to move out of the mansion their possessions, such as china and clothing.

One of the china platters said to have been carried away in haste that day was not broken, and is owned now by a member of the Henry family.

At the time of this writing, *Genesar* mansion is like a huge dilapidated coffin stuffed with straw. It is used as a barn, and hay sticks out of doors and windows (p. 35). Except for building materials of old wood and brick, its monetary value is nothing. The roofs are caving in by degrees. For several years some floors were overloaded with bags of fertilizer and other farm materials, and fell in; other floors have been ripped up for sport. Brick partitions have been demolished by hand by visitors of a certain type. The carved spandrels on the side of the graceful stairway which rises to the attic have been systematically stripped down to the very last one (p. 33). All the doors and windows of the original house, except the broken pieces of one door found buried in fragments in the refuse of the attic, have disappeared from the premises. What a picture to paint for Marylanders and for that vast hinterland of persons interested in early American arts. Gradually, year by year, for more than twenty-two years, *Genesar* has been dying by inches—if a building with such a personality can die. It is now a shambles, beyond hope of repair or restoration, unless a fortune is spent upon it. And all these changes have been taking place—at least in recent years—with the main

A reconstruction drawing by the author, of GENESAR (c.1732), Worcester County, a Transitional mansion showing "the richest glazed brick patterns in the State."

paved highway to a new multi-million-dollar-beach development project running past the front door.

However that may be, the crowning indignity to *Genesar* came one dark night years ago—some time within that decade following 1941—when vandals pillaged the place. Now, a vandal is defined as a ruthless plunderer, a wilful destroyer of what is beautiful or artistic; and that description fits these particular visitors. It has been reported by several persons of the neighborhood, including the caretaker of the farm, that a truck was driven up to the house and the handsome paneling in the Hall Chamber, over the Hall or Great Room, was stripped from the walls and loaded. As may be seen in the photographs (p. 32), this paneling rose to the ceiling on three sides. That the murky deed was a hasty one is indicated by the fact that the thieves left significant pieces of the woodwork behind them.

Pilfered at that time or at another was the dining-room cupboard in the style of Queen Anne, with scrolled shelves, as well as most of the woodwork in that room and in the Great Room. The dining-room mantelpiece had pilasters with

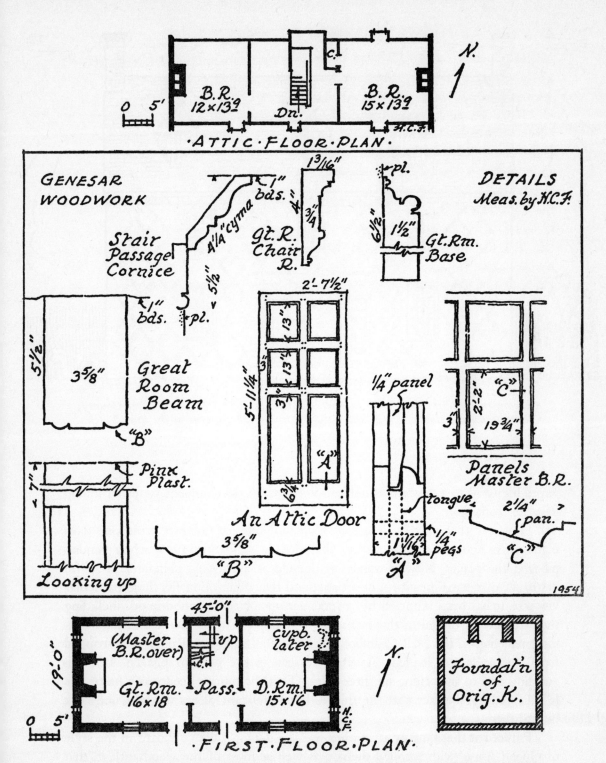

·ATTIC·FLOOR·PLAN·

B.R.
12×13½

Dn.

B.R.
15×13½

N.
1

0 5'

H.C.F.

GENESAR
WOODWORK

DETAILS
Meas. by H.C.F.

Stair
Passage
Cornice

4¼" cyma

1"
bds.

Gt. R.
Chair
R.

1³/₁₆"

4"

3"
4"

pl.

6½"

1½"

Gt. Rm.
Base

5½"

1"
bds.

pl.

2'-7½"

13"

13"

3"

3"

3"

5'-11¼"

¼ panel

3"

2'-2"

"C"

19¾"

5½"

3⅝"

Great
Room
Beam

"B"

An Attic Door

tongue

¼"
pegs

1¹/₁₆"

"A"

Panels
Master B.R.

2¼"
pan.

"C"

7"

Pink
Plast.

3⅝"

Looking up

"B"

"A"

1954

(Master
B.R. over)

45'-0"

up

H.C.F.

cupb.
later

N.
1

19'-0"

Gt. Rm.
16×18

Pass.

D. Rm.
15×16

Foundat'n
of
Orig. K.

0 5'

H.C.F.

·FIRST·FLOOR·PLAN·

The original floor plans and some woodwork details of GENESAR. Note the double
doors on front and back, and the four attic dormers.

sunken panels and a rope molding around the opening. Some of the paneled pilasters on pedestals which framed the windows in the Great Room are still in place —overlooked by the marauders. After all, it is not easy to work fast by flashlight.

It has been reported in the neighborhood that the paneling from the Hall Chamber now stands with elegance in a home in a neighboring state; but wherever it is, Maryland has lost probably its foremost example of Transitional woodwork. In its design of small squares and near-squares this paneling forms the intermediate step between the earlier, random-width, vertical boarding, which is Medieval, and the large, rectangular-designed panels which are Georgian. In truth it is difficult to locate any other paneled room in this country like that at *Genesar*.

The slenderness of the main block is distinctive: forty-five feet long by nineteen feet wide, and two and a half storeys high. There is no basement. The house towers skyward like a chimney stack, an excellent example of the Tran-

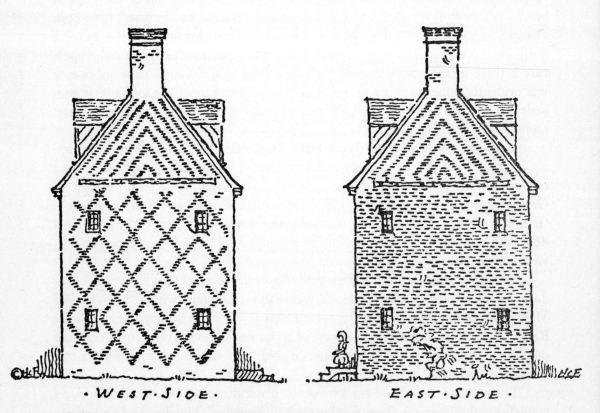

· WEST · SIDE ·   EAST · SIDE ·

Gable-end reconstructions of GENESAR. Here "Maryland loses the most interesting building of the Transitional Style of Architecture."

sition, where the blossoming has taken place upward instead of rearward (p. 31). The roof is steep, and had at one time four dormers, only one of which now remains (p. 36). Even so, it is scarcely an exaggeration to declare that this lone dormer on the back roof is the most steeply-pointed early one in Maryland. The eaves of the main roof "kicked" or "swallowtailed" outward by means of a system of wooden wedges fastened upon the lower ends of the rafters. The main cornice on the front is an early Georgian type, carrying S-shaped modillions, dentils, and a bed molding of recessed elliptical arches, alternately small and large. At the ends of this front cornice the modillions return on themselves. Between the modillions runs a punctate design of the same elliptical-arch motif noted above. All in all, the Purnell builder with this ornamental cornice put his best foot foremost, because the rear cornice is a plain, box-like affair. Another detail of interest is the barge board with cyma molding filling the space under the edge of the cedar shingles at the rake.

The charm of the early style lies largely in its details, and one of these details was the insertion of four tiny windows in each gable end of the original block. All these eight openings, as far as present research has disclosed, have been changed in size or blocked up in one way or another. Further, there is today a ninth small opening, a lie-on-your-stomach window, in the west gable. This aperture is three inches wider than any of the others and, although early in date, it was evidently punched through the brick wall to give ventilation to the west attic bedroom, which had only one dormer. Consequently, this window has been omitted in the drawings (p. 8).

In doing what amounted to detective work upon the front and rear façades, we found that the house originally had two front doors and two back doors, where today there exists only one door in each front. At some period in the history of *Genesar* mansion two doors were changed into windows; now that the window frames have been stripped from the walls, the door-head timbers of the original doorways may be seen embedded in the masonry walls—enough evidence to convince the most skeptical investigator.

When the dwelling was first erected, the Great Room had a front and a rear doorway all to itself, features which were later made into windows. Why did Major John Purnell need so many outside doors? There is no trace of the Great Room having been the downstairs part of an earlier domicile; then for what were double doors in front and back? Symmetry? Early American architecture is not without its puzzles.

The most ornate glazed brickwork, or black diapering, known in Maryland embellishes the front façade and gable ends of *Genesar*. The diamond or lozenge pattern in brick is called black diapering in England, where it was widespread in the early sixteen century. The tracing out of the glazed brickwork at *Genesar* under a heavy coat of stucco has been a far more difficult task than the drawings indicate; but enough evidence was found to make the reconstructions. Curiously enough, less of the patterns beneath the stucco may be seen at the site than from certain photographs, which, Xray-like, reveal the designs. Where no evidence was to be had, we have put in the designs conjecturally.

The lozengy, or design in diamonds, covers the west gable end below the string course or fascia, above which are inverted Vs or chevrons. This gable resembles that at *Make Peace* in Somerset County, Maryland, but is one storey taller. Perhaps the gable at *Quinn* or *Sweet Air*, Baltimore County, comes close to the west gable end of *Genesar*, but it does not have the chevrons. The main front of *Genesar* resembles the diapering at *Fassit House*, Worcester County, a smaller home of one and a half storeys. The north gable of *Genesar* keeps above the string course the chevrons of the south gable but, below it, lapses into ordinary Flemish bond with glazed headers (p. 36). There was no need in the builder's mind to place an elaborate lozengy opposite the kitchen dependency, which stood only seventeen feet away from the gable end.

The stucco which covers the main block was put on during the nineteenth century, and was lightly grooved or scored to represent ashlar masonry. At that time, possibly the 1860s or '70s, there was a small front porch shading the remaining front doorway. The column marks of this porch are still visible against the windows which flank this doorway. Also there are crude traces of the roof crossing the lower corner of a second floor window—a Victorian peculiarity. One puzzling feature of the existing front door is the two-inch-deep groove in the brickwork above it (p. 35). The other doorway on the front appears to have had a similar incision in the brick wall. That the hollow shows no signs of chiseling of the masonry would indicate that the groove was made when the walls were first built; but its purpose is a mystery. The groove is not deep enough to support a hood over the doorway.

Some other features of the interior are of note. On the first floor ceiling are wide flat boards, characteristic of houses of this section of Worcester County. On closer investigation, it was found that the boards had been nailed over decorative beams which were once exposed. Each beam is edged with rounded moldings, flattened out in what may be called an un-Gothic manner. Possibly such moldings, which are shown on the drawings, may be termed Transitional. At any rate, these moldings in each beam stop abruptly, without lamb's tongues, at a distance of seven inches from the plaster wall.

The Great Room has pink plaster, possibly the original color—although Victorians well liked pink—and, before the walls were stripped, it had an elaborate trim of pilasters flanking the windows. Also the chair rail and baseboard are very curvilinear. On the stairway the balusters were plain, having been rectangular in section. The spandrels were elaborately carved with pierced scrolls somewhat in the shape of a question mark. Below the spandrels runs a flat band of incised stub flutes, making a pattern. The side of the stair is paneled. But most of all these features are going or gone.

The present brick kitchen, and "the curtain" or passageway connecting it with the main block, are additions of the nineteenth century. After spending an hour or so in the cramped crawl-in space under the kitchen—an area full of dead spiders, snakes, skeletons, trash, cobwebs, and dirt—we came to the conclusion that the kitchen foundation, built of larger bricks than those of the present kitchen, is original, and formerly supported a wooden building of perhaps 1732. Be that as it may, there was found no evidence of a "curtain" to the main house in the eighteenth century; and the food must have been carried out of doors to the back door in the stair passage of the main house and from thence to the dining room. Small wonder that in the early days silver platter covers and padded tea cozies were necessary.

The kitchen development at *Genesar* has been worked out something like this: first, a separate frame kitchen dependency; second, the present nineteenth-century kitchen erected on the foundation of the original, and a brick curtain built simultaneously the full width of the main house. This curtain was roofed with a flat deck which sloped downward toward the rear and crossed one of the tiny end windows of the east gable end. Two doors were cut in the east gable end for access to the main house: one, downstairs, to shorten the food route to the dining room; the other, opening upon a flat deck from the second-floor east bedroom. Why the owners needed to go out on the flat deck is perplexing. In those days bathing beauties did not lie prone on open decks for suntan; third, the rear brick wall of the curtain was taken down, or it collapsed, and a new frame wall built which very much narrowed the passageway. The roof was changed to a pitched one. This is the curtain as it exists today.

By 1932, the year of our first visit, the *Genesar* tombstones had disappeared. The dilapidated smoke house with an interesting overhang and a rough battened door swinging on strap hinges still stood, a good bull's eye for Father Time. By now, all the outbuildings of *Genesar* have disappeared. But when the remaining bricks and timbers of the mansion house have been finally carried away to make room for a real-estate development, Maryland will possess only a few photographs and drawings of what was perhaps its most outstanding example of the Transitional Style of architecture and of what was one of the most unique early edifices of this nation.

2. *SANDY POINT* OF THE DANCING FLOOR

A BRICK SHELL of its former self, *Sandy Point*, or Dirickson House, is not to be confused with *Little Sandy Point* nearby. Both houses are situated in Sinepuxent Neck, Worcester County. An old photograph of *Sandy Point* is here reproduced, along with our reconstructed floor plan (pp. 15, 37).

This plantation house, according to Mrs. Ethan Allen Carey, a local authority, was built a little before 1812 by John Ratcliff, a man who was killed by his slaves. Even before the scaffolding had been removed, the mansion was burned by the English in the War of 1812. It was then rebuilt within the brick walls. Later the farm came into the possession of John C. Dirickson, who left it to his son, James Brevard Dirickson, the uncle of Mrs. Ethan Allen Carey. James Dirickson was a graduate of Trinity College, Hartford, and lived most of his life at *Sandy Point*. He never married, but maintained colored servants to run the place. Afterwards, Mrs. Carey and her two brothers, who were also the owners of *Genesar*, kept the farm for over twenty years. She remembers that the large parlor, or Great Room, faced the woods and the long lane, and had a springy floor, which, she was told as a child, was built for dancing. The room back of the main stairway was used for a storeroom, and the other room on the ocean side was the dining room, off which the brick kitchen wing extends. Downstairs there were three splendid catercornered fireplaces with marble mantels. Probably a fourth fireplace stood in the room used for stores in order to make a balanced and shipshape plan. There were four bedrooms upstairs, as well as a large attic at the top of the house.

Outside at front and back, formerly stood small porches, probably not original. The existing brick walls of the dwelling are now covered with a smooth stucco having incised lines to imitate dressed stonework, like that done at *Genesar*, *Burley Manor*, and other buildings of this area. Around the main block there is a chamfered water table, and the cellar has been filled in. Taking one thing with another, the homestead has been so much changed that its original lines, both inside and out, have largely disappeared.

The larger size of brick in the kitchen wing indicates to this writer that this section comprised the first house, possibly built before the American Revolution. Then the main block must have been the addition, probably erected, as Mrs. Carey has indicated, a little before 1812. The water table of the kitchen wing is different from that of the main block and comprises two brick steps.

The plantation originally had, among numerous outbuildings, a well house, a barn, a quarters, and cowsheds with a pound or enclosure. Some of these structures show in the old photograph.

3. *BURLEY MANOR*, GARDEN SPOT OF THE 1830s

THIS SMALL plantation forms an excellent example of how an Eastern Shore gentleman lived in the fourth decade of the nineteenth century and, further, how the maximum economic efficiency was obtained thereon by means of careful planning and of layout of grounds and buildings—having in mind, at the same time, the beauty of both.

The brick dwelling house (p. 39) was erected in 1832-33 by John Mitchell and was called *Burley Manor*, after the land on which it stands. Undoubtedly the original tract gave the name to the town of Berlin, in which the homestead stands; and consequently the name of the town bears the accent on the first syllable—that is, except by telephone operators and others who pronounce it like the name of the former capital of Germany.

We find that on June 22, 1677, Colonel William Stevens of Somerset County had deeded unto him 300 acres of land called Burley. These acres were later assigned by Stevens to William Tomkins, for which Tomkins received a patent on July 12, 1683.

Burley, which is spelled Bourly in the Tomkins patent, lay on the "Seaboard side, about three miles back in the woods from the salt water of the sea near the head of Assateague River"—the present Trappe Creek, which runs into Newport Bay. It is interesting that one of the boundaries of the property was a white oak standing on the side of a "Savanna."

At present *Burley Manor* comprises about forty-five acres. It was probably called "Manor" to distinguish it from *Burley Cottage*, which stands within sight of it.

In 1833 or thereabouts, Mrs. Elizabeth Hammond, *née* Victor, the widow of Edward Hammond of Queponco, purchased *Burley Manor* from John Mitchell, and into it moved herself and her family of four small children. Queponco, by the way, is an interesting section of Worcester County, lying on the east side of the Pocomoke River, where the Hammonds since 1677 had lived.

There is some justification in calling *Burley Manor* the Hammond House, because ever since the widow Elizabeth Hammond moved into it a century and a quarter ago the home has been owned and occupied by members of the family of that name.

Upon Elizabeth Hammond's death, *Burley Manor* descended to her only surviving child, Dr. John Taylor Hammond, a graduate of the Jefferson Medical College in Philadelphia. He married Esther Priscilla Toadvine and served many years as a country doctor—one with the kindest of hearts—until his death in 1902. It was his custom to go out at night to visit the sickest of his patients, such as those with typhoid fever, of whom he is said never to have lost a case. Regardless of how bad was the weather, he would drive many miles, often over roads which were little better than quagmires. On his return home he would sometimes find a person from the locality from which he had just come who wanted him to visit a sick member of that person's family. At any rate, without a murmur, off would go the good doctor on another trip through the darkness.

In order to lessen this burden of mileage, he planned two innovations, one after the other. At first he commenced the practice of going up to every house in the particular locality where he happened to be, at a goodly distance from home, and of asking the occupants, who stood sleepily around in nightgowns and night-caps whether or not there was any person sick there. But especially because of the opening and closing of gates in the lanes in which he travelled, the physician found this plan too much of a hardship. So he tried another plan, that of asking anyone who had a sick member in his family to place a light in the window. This scheme worked.

No matter how far he went at night in his buggy, his charge for a visit was usually one dollar. Besides, the dollar included medicine made by Dr. Hammond himself.

Very often he would furnish food which had been specially prepared at home to such of his patients as he thought required it. To those who were unable to pay for it, this food was free. He never sent out any bills, because he believed that whoever owed him anything would pay him when able to do so. Further, this remarkable man signed the note of any person who asked him to sign; unfortunately he had to pay many of the notes on which he had put his signature. One of his sons, Dr. Thomas Victor Hammond, who, after less than a year's practice with his father, Dr. John T. Hammond, had moved to the city of Washington to practice there, realized that this custom of his father of signing other people's notes would eventually result in the loss by his father of all his property, of which there was a great deal and from which his father received practically no income. Thereupon the son suggested to his father that the father's two unmarried daughters, Kate and Virginia Hammond, be deeded all the family property. But his father was up in arms at once and refused to listen to the suggestion, saying that if he deeded away all his possessions, no longer would anyone ask him to sign a note. But eventually, his father conveyed all his possessions to his two daughters, and *Burley Manor* became secure.

Dr. Thomas Victor Hammond, son of this father of good deeds, married

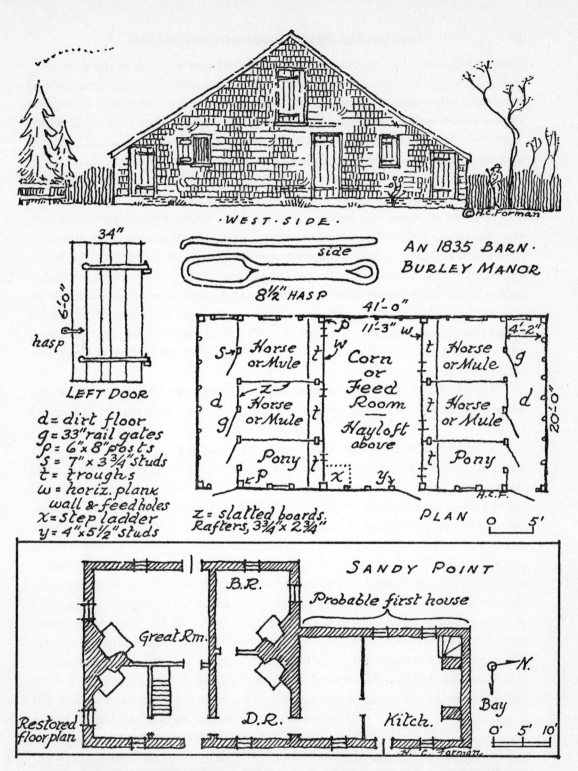

·WEST·SIDE·

©H.C.Forman

side

8½" HASP

AN 1835 BARN·
BURLEY MANOR

34"

6'-0"

hasp

LEFT DOOR

d = dirt floor
g = 33" rail gates
p = 6" x 8" posts
s = 7" x 3¾" studs
t = troughs
w = horiz. plank
     wall & feedholes
x = step ladder
y = 4" x 5½" studs

z = slatted boards.
Rafters, 3¾" x 2¾"

41'-0"

11'-3" w

4'-2"

S→ Horse
    or Mule   t w   Corn
                       or
z   Horse   Feed
       or Mule   Room

d
g   — Hayloft
                       above —

Pony   P   x   y

t   Horse
     or Mule

t

t   Horse
     or Mule

g

d

t   Pony

20'-0"

H.C.F.

PLAN   0   5'

SANDY POINT

B.R.

Great Rm.

Probable first house

N.

Bay

D.R.   Kitch.

Restored
floor plan

H. C. Forman

0'   5'   10'

The BURLEY MANOR BARN, built in 1835 in Berlin, Worcester County, is faced
with shingles; below, the reconstructed floor plan of SANDY POINT or DIRICKSON
HOUSE, Worcester County, once the home of a wealthy bachelor.

Bertha Hopkins of Washington, D.C. He occupied the family homestead at *Burley Manor* in the summertime, until about 1920, when he retired there.[1]

Burley Manor fronts on Main Street in Berlin, and it formerly had a "pale" or picket fence (p. 41) around the front lawn—now replaced by a privet hedge. A small gate used to open upon a long brick path, still in evidence, leading through the front yard of grass and great trees to the front porch. There are cedars, some of which are now dead and covered with ivy, lindens, maples, sycamores, firs, locusts, walnuts and mimosas. The front porch (p. 40) covers the front door and leaves the windows of the front parlor clear for light and ventilation. The porch columns taper, with entasis, and the Doric caps are squeezed thin. The segmental arches have a kind of dog-tooth ornament, reminiscent of the Romanesque. There are sunbursts and quarter sunbursts, as well as modillions. The board ceiling of the porch is painted sky blue.

The front door is wide—three feet and seven inches—and there are twelve molded panels upon it. The jambs of the doorway are eighteen inches wide and paneled. Above is a fanlight, having not the usual panes set in muntins but a large sheet of glass with the muntins set up against it. One unusual feature of the front doorway is the double jalousied or slatted screen doors, opening out, painted green and used in summertime.

Once inside, you find a long passageway divided in the middle by an archway to form a front and a back hall. Undoubtedly by 1833 the term "hall" no longer referred to the Great Hall or Great Room, but to the passageway in a house. This hall leads to a rear door which opens onto the porch facing the garden. Moreover, on the left side of the hallway are doors to front and back parlor and, on the right, the doorway to the dining room, which is in a small, separate wing. Over the doors are square-headed transoms for light and ventilation.

The two parlors are separated by an arch with wide sliding doors which disappear into the partition. The main stairway rises from the back part of the hall and has a mahogany rail and elaborately-scrolled spandrels. Upstairs the passage opens upon four bedrooms, two of which are of interest: the Parlor Chamber over the front parlor, used as a guest room, and the Lower Room over the dining room, so-called because it has one step down from the passage. In 1833 there appears to have been no central heating in use in this region—although the *Villa* in Talbot County, built only nineteen years later, had a furnace with ducts—and consequently all the rooms of *Burley Manor* have fireplaces.

[1] Upon the death of Thomas Victor Hammond in 1942, *Burley Manor* became the property of his son, Edward Hopkins Hammond, who, with his wife, the former Grace Powell of Atlanta, Georgia, and their two children, Ann Powell and Edward Hopkins, Jr., now occupy the dwelling house. These two are the fifth generation, in direct line to occupy *Burley Manor*.

The third floor, located under the roof of the main block, has two finished rooms lighted by large gable windows. There are capacious closets under the eaves. Above the third floor is an attic with a stepladder reaching to a trap door in the roof.

The kitchen is gained by a passage from the dining room and forms, along with the slave's bedroom above it, a low brick wing at right angles to the dining-room wing and picturesquely joined to it. In this kitchen is an arched fireplace, almost big enough to take a five-foot log, flanked by a cupboard on one side and a small staircase on the other. There has been some question as to whether the kitchen was built at a different time from the rest of the house. It is almost impossible to study the outside brickwork of this kitchen because of a coat of stucco over the whole house, a coat probably put on after the Civil War. But if the woodwork of the kitchen is any indication, the whole abode was built simultaneously. The stucco, it appears, was incised with lines to imitate ashlar masonry. Over the windows the mason formed hollow stucco flat arches, in order to emphasize the brick arches underneath.

Originally the roof was covered with cypress shingles, averaging two and a half feet long, hand-hewn from very old trees found in the Pocomoke River. These shingles lasted for over a hundred years.

In the brick cellar, under the main block, there are three rooms, the smallest with a brick floor having been used as the milk room. Here was a hanging shelf the full length of the room. Crocks lining this shelf were poured in rotation, after the morning and evening milkings, so that the milk would always be fresh. The cream formed was used for the table and for making butter. In another basement room there used to hang a food shelf, protected by wire netting—the early refrigerator.

At the rear of the main house lies the garden with its numerous appurtenances; and off the kitchen, a group of farm buildings. As may be seen from the plot plan (p. 18), the garden is not arranged in the classical manner of symmetry and formality, like the great Georgian gardens, but in a romantic, informal fashion. Even though the dwelling is largely Hangover Georgian in style, the garden layout is not.

From the rear or garden porch, which is partly paved with brick for coolness in summertime, a broad path leads along the axis of the flower garden and through a large vegetable garden. The left-hand portion of the flower garden is twice as large as the right-hand part—an arrangement making an informal balance. Besides, the serpentine path which once meandered through clumps of shrubs, flower beds, and mimosa trees, in the direction of the brick greenhouse, gave a delightfully informal note to the over-all design.

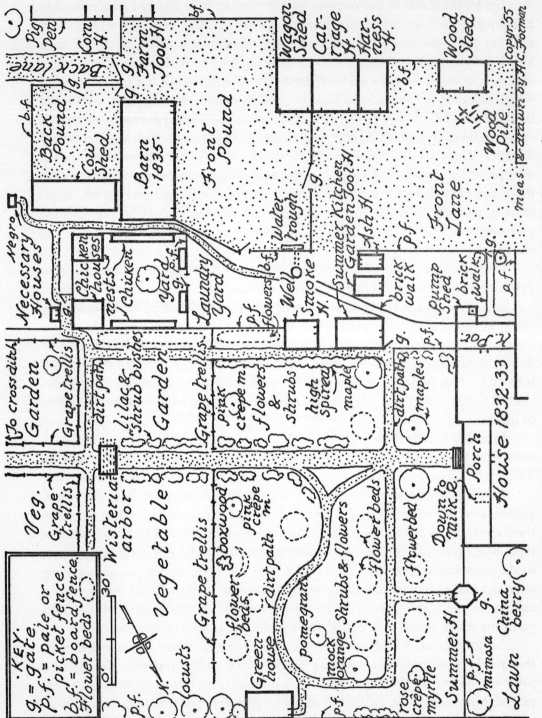

The garden and farmyard (restored) plan of *BURLEY MANOR* illustrates how nearly everything necessary to life was grown or manufactured on the place.

Under the shade of the trees on humid summer days one can inhale the delicate odor of the roses, which dominate the flower garden. There are several varieties, but the moss rose is a special. Among the shrubs is crêpe myrtle of three
kinds—purple, pink, and rose-color—all growing high enough to set off the lower
shrubs. Among other flowers and shrubs are the flowering red quince, two of
which bloom in winter; snowballs; variegated boxwood; double yellow corchorus;
the Japanese globeflower; light-red weigela; white and blue hydrangeas; and spirea,
of which there are four different types, the most common of which is called "bridal
wreath." There are also mock orange, wisteria, forsythia, a tartarian honeysuckle,
a purple-lily magnolia, and a rare pomegranate bush which does not bear fruit. In
the olden days there were three oleanders of different colors and a pink, single
camelia, each set in a tub so that in winter these plants could be put into the
greenhouse or the cellar. Among the garden trees are the mimosa, maple, and
chinaberry.

On the north side of the house, separating the flower garden from the front
yard once stood an open, octagonal summerhouse, with a gate at the front and a
seat inside big enough for two. A finial crowned a roof covered with white roses
and crimson ramblers. Separating the flower garden from the vegetable garden
once stood a trellis of grapevines. Beyond this trellis and standing a little way
down the path forming the main axis was a rectangular arbor, without seats. It was
held up by four posts and covered with wisteria. Everywhere about were whitewashed picket fences and gates to separate one enclosure from another, according
to its use.

In addition to the grapes from which jellies, jams, and wines were made, there
were fruit trees, some of which still exist: apple, peach, cherry, plum and the like.
There were also abundant strawberries, raspberries, blackberries, and gooseberries.

At the side of the kitchen porch, and carefully kept apart from the whole
garden area by a long picket fence to keep out chickens and other livestock,
there stood in the heyday of *Burley Manor* at least sixteen outbuildings. None of
these were dependencies, because in composition they did not flank or appertain
to the main house. But they did form a small village of structures, each serving
some definite purpose and helping to make this small plantation a self-economic
unit, in an age when there were no telephones, electric lights, supermarkets, department stores, canning factories, automobiles, jet planes, or television sets.

At one side of the kitchen porch and its attached, latticed, pump shed is an
area partly paved with herringbone brick, which today might be designated a
patio or courtyard. On the other side are three small out-structures, neatly arranged with their front gables in line. The largest is the frame summer kitchen
which has a little knock-head in the loft for a slave; the middle-sized one is the

wooden garden tool house; and the little one is the brick ash house used for storing wood ashes. These ashes came originally from the fireplaces of the house, in later times from stoves, and they were scattered over the gardens and fields each spring-time. The ash house itself (p. 191) is only eight feet and nine inches long. It comprises a duplex, with an open doorway at each end and a low brick partition across the middle allowing for ventilation.

At the back of the summer kitchen, off the laundry yard, is the smoke house for smoking and preserving meats. It is constructed of heavy planks and decorated at the corners with fish-scale shingles. Inside are the hearth, a chopping table, and two large iron pots in which water was boiled at hog-killing time.

In the laundry yard and next to the Front Pound was the well, reached from the kitchen porch by a brick walk. Water was drawn and poured into a V-board channel to a log water trough inside the Front Pound. At this log trough thirsty horses, mules, and ponies would refresh themselves upon returning from the fields or town—provided, of course, there was a slave to draw water and tip the buckets. Dominating the Front Pound is the old barn (pp. 40), which had in it a brick bearing the date 1835. This structure is part barn—having a corn or feed room downstairs and hayloft above, reached by a stepladder through a little square open-ing—and part stable—having three stalls on each side for horses, mules, and ponies. The barn itself is frame faced with small shingles, and has batten doors and batten window shutters supported on strap hinges.

Also lining the Front Pound was the wagon shed, no longer there, which formed an extension on one side of the carriage house, and the farm tool house. From the rear of the Front Pound a tree-lined lane led past the Back Pound, which opened onto the cow shed, and past the log corn house and the pigpen—both of which have felt the effects of Father Time and vanished—and ran across the fields to the woods.

Perhaps the locations of these outbuildings and their pounds seem compli-cated to the reader, but a study of the plot plan will make their arrangements clear. We come next to the chicken yard, now gone, which was situated between the vegetable garden and the barn, and was rectangular and bounded entirely by a pale fence about sixteen feet high. In the center of the chicken yard is a paulownia tree. It is interesting to learn that each pale of this high fence, built to keep out foxes and other chicken-loving animals and to keep the chickens in, was cut at the top into a V, so that, when placed contiguous to one another, the pales made sharp points. Inside the enclosure, on three sides, stood four-foot poles holding up nesting platforms, on the top of which were adjoining boxes with pitched roofs. In the back of the enclosure were two separate houses where the chickens roosted and kept warm.

Back of the chicken yard area stands the white "necessary" house; its black counterpart, off the end of the cow shed, was used by the slaves.

In the broad part of the front lane, opposite the kitchen porch and next to the Front Pound, stands the carriage house, now quite weatherbeaten, covered with fish-scale shingles thirty inches long, which show about eleven inches to the weather. The wagon shed was on one side of the carriage house on the inside of the Front Pound, as mentioned above, and on the other side stands the harness house, where the tack for the riding and driving horses were kept and where the groom slept in a back room. Near the harness house, now used as a garage, and bordering the front lane is the wood pile where hog killing took place. Back of the wood pile there used to stand a wood shed about sixteen feet long, separated into two compartments, one for wood, the other for coal.

All the outbuildings of this small village were whitewashed, and red paint was employed on the doors, windows, gates, and roofs. At a distance from the residence and its farm group stood various slave quarters, one of which is still standing on the edge of the highway leading southward.

The cows were milked in the Back Pound, and the milk, instead of being taken to a dairy house, for there was none, was carried down through the cellar areaway in the back or garden porch of the house to the milk room, and kept in jugs on a shelf, as described. Spinning was done on wheels in the summer kitchen, in the regular kitchen, and on the third floor of the house.

Nearly everything necessary to life was made right on the property, and there were plenty of slaves to do manual labor.

4. TIME AND MAN AT THE *SAMUEL ADAMS HOUSE*

THOSE MUSEUM PEOPLE and antique dealers who search for old buildings to strip will probably be disappointed in this little plantation house hidden away behind the pine forests of the Lower Eastern Shore. In 1951 we found this place and made preliminary notes about it. Returning three years later, we had to face the fact that complete measurements would never be made, because the paneling, woodwork, stairway, and floors had been removed a little while before.

The *Samuel Adams House* (pp. 42, 73) is a brick, one-storey-and-a-half habitation with basement, and was erected five years before the end of the eighteenth century. On the brick walls is carved "S A 1795." The kitchen wing and curtain, of frame, are of later date, and now stand at the point of collapse.

One enters the house by a Victorian front porch with a sunray tympanum which leads into a narrow stair passage along the east gable end. The Great Room is on the left and has a catercornered fireplace. At the rear are two cells or aisles, one back of the stair passage, the other behind the Great Room. This latter cell was used as a dining room; it too has a diagonal fireplace. Between the two cells is a vertical-board partition.

Upstairs there is a narrow passageway running longitudinally across the house —that is, beneath the ridge pole. Three bedrooms give on this passage. There are no dormers, because each room is lighted by a small window in the gable. But the most curious feature of the second floor is the cubbyhole, with door, located at the west end of the narrow passageway and jammed up against the chimney. This tiny space contains a stepladder to a supra-attic or loft-above-loft, which is lit by a single lie-on-your-stomach window.

Here, in the decaying *Samuel Adams House*, built almost at the very threshold of the nineteenth century, is a "stee" or ladder, earliest type of medieval stairway of Britain.

Before the removal of its woodwork, the Great Room had a low wainscoting and a reeded mantel, marked by a band of horizontal reeded ovals. The skirting or base was marbleized, and the panels were grained—that is, decorated with imitation-woodwork graining in paint. The Great Room doors—one to the stair passage, the other to the dining room—had rectangular panels painted in ovals simulating inlay work.

In spite of this Federal sophisticated ornament on the interior, in style the dwelling is technically Hangover Transitional of the Late Cell type. This means that it has cells at the rear, although the gables are symmetrical, and that it is an example of an earlier type persisting very late into the eighteenth century. For all that, the front door, now gone, was Hangover Medieval in style. It was a batten door hanging by strap hinges and had vertical random-width boards with a quarter-round molding between each board.

What a pity that all these details were removed before they could be properly recorded by measurements and photographs. Nothing is truer than the maxim that the time to do a thing is now. Our three-year delay in returning to this haunt prevented a complete study.

5. THE FIRST DIAMOND STACKS, AT
THE REWARD

ONE OF THE RARE finds in Maryland came two years ago when this writer came upon *The Reward* (p. 43), which has the only early diamond stacks known in the State. What is almost as unusual as the discovery itself is that the date of these chimney stacks is as late as 1794, if the carving on the kitchen chimney is an indication.

The diamond stack, meaning a chimney stack or shaft set diagonally on its base, originated in medieval England. In the late sixteenth century, it seems the usual chimney stacks were set square or diamond-like, and were built singly or in groups.[1] *The Reward* is fortunate in having both types of shaft on the main house —a single square stack on the west side, and twin diamonds on the east. Further, these chimneys were built on the side walls of the house and not on the gables, as was customary. But setting fireplaces on the side walls of a building is an old English medieval motif. It may be recalled that the first known examples of the medieval side chimney in the English colonies, as contrasted with the gable chimneys, occurred at the Country House and Ludwell I house at Jamestown, Virginia, about 1663.

The diamond stacks at *The Reward* are joined at the cap, as are similar shafts at *Bacon's Castle* (c.1650) and *Winona* (c.1700 or later) in Virginia; but they have no plinths or washes, which are sloping surfaces to cast off water, no necking bands, and no bases upon which to stand. The twin shafts simply disappear into the sloping roof. There is a large gusset, marked "g" on our drawing (p. 25), situated behind the stacks. Where the gusset abuts the shafts, a vertical board is placed against them in order to conceal the underside of the gusset. All in all, these diamond stacks may be designated the most naïvely designed early ones in the United States.

For several years this writer believed that sooner or later a Maryland diamond chimney would be discovered. In the old days Maryland and Virginia abounded with square and diamond shafts. For example, in St. Mary's County Governor Leonard Calvert owned the Piney Neck House, which was erected in 1642 with a stack of brick chimneys, containing two flues, situated in the middle of the dwelling. Still another structure of that time had "two stacks of brick chimneys."

The floor plan of *The Reward* is shown herewith (p. 25), drawn under various limitations. In the first place, the persons living there as caretakers were

[1] Forman, H. C., *The Architecture of the Old South*, Cambridge, Mass., 1948, p. 59.

adamant that no one could enter the house. When this writer after lengthy persuasion proved that his interest in the place was genuine, he was admitted into the forepart of the dwelling for five minutes. He could take measurements if he could get them in that period. He could not under any circumstances enter the kitchen-curtain wing.

If the reader has ever had the experience of taking accurate measurements of a building on the interior, he will know how rapidly he would have to work in order to obtain all the chief dimensions within a given five minutes. It was a case either of accepting the limitation imposed or of going without a floor plan. On our drawing the dotted lines show the kitchen fireplace, "said" to be eight feet long, located beside a winding staircase.

High up on the kitchen chimney were old characters—as far as could be ascertained, "A[NNO]1794." The kitchen seems to have been built at the same time as the main house. In fact, the entire plantation house, except perhaps the curtain or passageway and its little outshut, can be dated as 1794.

The main gable of the dwelling is broad, tall, and faces the water. There are several comparable examples of Eastern Shore homes with gables on the front, and they all run about 1785 or 1800 in date: *Goose Creek Farm* (c.1790), *Wye House* (c.1784), *Teackle Mansion* (c.1801), and *Finley Farm*, also known as *Kennersley* (c.1795-1800). At *The Reward* the first floor openings on the front have segmental brick arches. The upper gable, high and peaked, has clapboards across it like many a ranch house today; but originally it was probably brick all the way to the ridge pole. And there may have been an upper attic window.

The carved end-boards to the cornice are recent, so in the drawing we have designed them conjecturally. The floor plan with diagonal or catercornered fireplaces is similar to that of the other *Reward*, on Langford Bay, a much earlier building of the Transitional Style, dating from the beginning of the eighteenth century.

The Reward is not Georgian in style, but Federal or Early Republican, and the diamond stacks are examples of the Hangover Medieval Style in the very late eighteenth century.

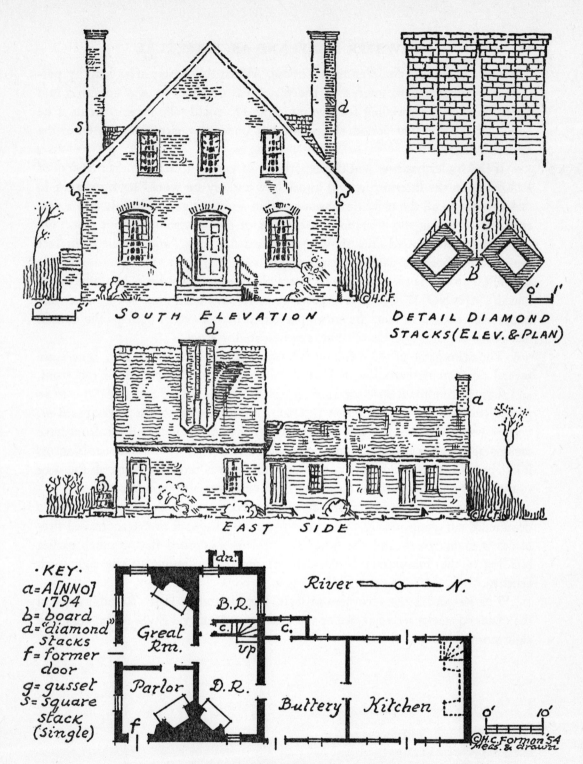

SOUTH ELEVATION

DETAIL DIAMOND
STACKS (ELEV. & PLAN)

EAST SIDE

·KEY·
a = A[NNO]
1794
b = board
d = "diamond"
stacks
f = former
door
g = gusset
s = square
stack
(single)

Great
Rm.

B.R.

up

Parlor   D.R.

Buttery   Kitchen

River   N.

Here the author has reconstructed THE REWARD on Eastern Shore, showing the
main gable facing the river and the twin diamond stacks on a long side. This dwelling
was a major discovery for the history of Southern architecture.

6. THE SPANISH DON'S BOXWOOD MAZE

ONE OF THE MOST beautiful yet least known box gardens in the Free State lies on the bank of Hurst Creek, a branch of the Choptank River, in Dorchester County. This is at the old plantation *El Don*, or *Eldon*, which belonged originally to Colonel Thomas Ennalls. The dwelling house in 1846 was destroyed by fire, and the notoriously handsome ballroom went up in smoke. The present house, on the same site, is now over one hundred years old.

While about two thirds of the great boxwood garden has been removed by the hand of man or by the waters of the river, which have eroded the shore, we have been able to secure enough data to make the enclosed measured garden plan (p. 27) after several trips to Cambridge. From the dwelling a walk, about 250 feet long, used to lead down to the box garden, laid out in twenty-seven rectangles and one circle, or oval. On the house side of the garden is a line of old cedar trees, which "lean against the wind" because of the prevailing breezes from the Choptank. The oval or circle lay at the end of the walk and contained a spiral maze, or labyrinth, made of box. Certainly this maze formed a tempting excursion for children and lovers; and there was no danger of getting lost in it.

The twenty-seven box squares—there are only portions of squares remaining—averaged forty-two feet on a side, and there were eight feet allowed for walks between the squares. The entire garden was enclosed with a border comprising two rows of boxwood set close together, and this border is drawn on the plan. As at *Perry Hall*, Talbot County, the flowers inside the squares were the important element in the design; the boxwood formed a small, low trim to them. But today the flowers have gone and the boxwood has grown gigantically (p. 44).

Within the memory of living men, there were no summerhouses, pergolas, or gates in the *El Don* garden; but originally there probably were such, because the Southern planter liked to ornament his garden in the English fashion.

According to tradition—and we must stress that it is only tradition—this property was named The Gift El Don, because one of the Ennalls girls is believed to have married a Spanish Don. Perhaps this legend is something a county historical society could investigate for the sake of accuracy.

After the Ennalls, the plantation was owned successively by members of the Bayard family, by James Billings Steele and his family, and by Dr. Francis Phelps, who erected the present dwelling house of 1846. The family graveyard stood a little to the west of this abode and contained, it is said, the stones of Colonel Henry Ennalls and Henry Wells. Some of the marble slabs from this venerable burial place, shaded by the great trees of the old park, were pitched into the river nearby.

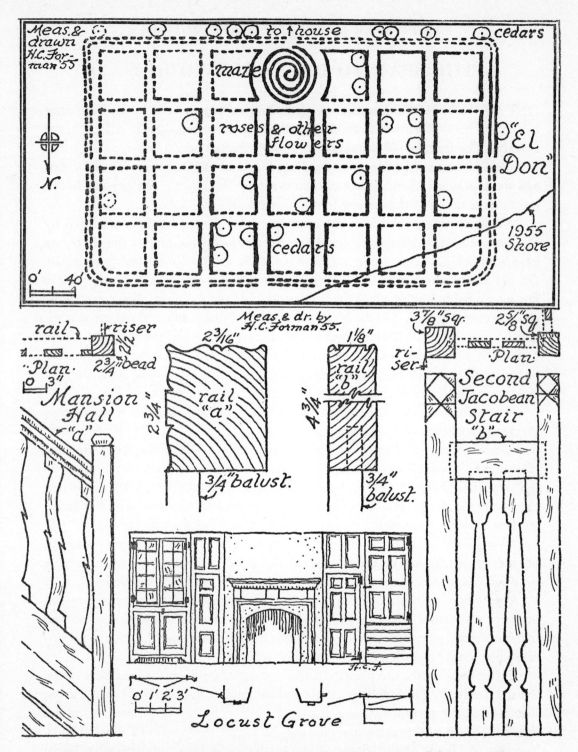

Above, *the writer's reconstructed plot plan of EL DON garden. Below,* two Maryland staircases of Jacobean Style, one in Charles County, the other on Eastern Shore; *the Great Room with china closet having Chippendale feet, at* LOCUST GROVE, *a Talbot County ruin.*

7. THE SECOND JACOBEAN STAIRCASE

INSIDE AN OLD building on the Eastern Shore we unexpectedly ran across the second Jacobean stair ever found in Maryland. Years ago the first one was found by this writer in *Mansion Hall*, Charles County (p. 27), and was illustrated in *The Architecture of the Old South*. The balusters at *Mansion Hall*—at least before the tenants chopped them up for firewood—were splat- or flat-shaped, cut out of boards with a jigsaw. Their effect was strange, giving a curved, zigzag appearance. The newel post was "shaped"—that is, the top was carved into a finial —and the handrail had Gothic moldings. All in all, the *Mansion Hall* stair is a good example of the Jacobean Style in this country.

Now this second stair (p. 27) located in a nameless building on the Eastern Shore, has at the attic level balusters of splat design different from those of *Mansion Hall*. In their flatness they have the silhouette of regular round balusters, which are in reality stubby Doric columns with caps and bases. There are only four balusters, as the photograph shows (p. 45). The two newel posts, of different thickness, have shaped finials, each with thirteen facets. The handrail has no Gothic profile, but is beaded on the top at front and back. The balusters are pegged into the handrail and let into the floor boards.

Such is the design of this second stair of the Style of James I.

8. *FASSIT HOUSE* OF THE LABYRINTHIAN ZIGZAGS

IN 1932 THIS writer came upon *Fassit House* at the end of a muddy lane in the dead of winter. Plans, sketches, and photographs of it were first published in *Early Manor and Plantation Houses of Maryland*, and later in *The Architecture of the Old South*. Pictures of the dwelling now appear in department-store calendars and garden-club guides. The "duck" newel, which this writer named, has now become famous.

In the *Old South* volume it is stated that *Fassit House* is an example of the central-passage type persisting into the eighteenth century. The present owners have had the place renovated, building not too successfully a chimney on the west gable, following marks of a former chimney in the brickwork. The ancient kitchen and the catercornered fireplace in the dining room have not been restored.

The Great Room, which the writer was not permitted to enter on the day of "discovery" in 1932, has now been well repaired and reconditioned. It is a chamber which is paneled on one side to the ceiling (p. 46). The west windows in the brick gable end have been opened up, letting more light into the Great Room. Of note are the narrow pilasters resting on the wooden trim around the fireplace, the Wall-of-Troy molding in the cornice, and the large-size double dog-ears in the door and window trim. There is the usual wide-board ceiling found in this part of Maryland.

In the first volume noted above, it is written that "perhaps the glazed labyrinthian zigzags of *Fassit House* bring to a culmination the Southern love of play for its own sake as shown in the brickwork." This statement was paraphrased in the booklet entitled, *First Annual Pilgrimage of Old Homes and Landmarks in Berlin, Worcester County, Maryland* (1953), as follows: "It has been said the Colonial Builder liked to give his love of color and vivid display free reign in gay and complicated brickwork. *Fassit House* is the best example of this in Maryland." Nevertheless, in *The Architecture of the Old South,* published previous to 1953, this theory of gay brickwork was exploded. We showed that the Colonial builder copied his lozengy, or black diapering, from English architecture, which by the sixteenth century made universal use of the complicated pattern in glazed brick. The most famous structure in England possessing black diapering is Hampton Court Palace, built by Cardinal Wolsey.

Besides, lozengy was no monopoly of Southerners; and we find good examples of the use in some of the brick homes of New Jersey. As for *Fassit House,* we have stated that medieval black diapering continues in the eighteenth century upon its walls. And *Fassit House* is not the best example of such decoration in Maryland.

The Kitchen Porch, six feet deep, with sand floor, "San Domingo"

The west gable-end of GENESAR, in which lozengy may be seen by keen eyes, is marked by strong Gothic verticality. Author, 1934.

The rare Transitional panelling of the "Hall Chamber" at GENESAR, Worcester County, was secretly stolen and loaded into a truck in the night. Note the squares, near-squares, and door double-cross design. Author, 1934.

A detail of the handsome stair at GENESAR, before the "question-mark" spandrels on the steps were stripped. Author, 1934.

The approach front of GENESAR, Worcester County, as it looked in 1932, before much pillaging had been done. The well has now gone. Author.

A detail of the front wall and modillion cornice of GENESAR, now used as a barn. Note the curious groove in the brickwork over the front door. Below, view from dining room toward Great Room. Author, 1954.

The only one of four dormers at GENESAR has probably the steepest existing early peaked roof in Maryland. On east gable "chevrons" are visible. Below, a town box garden at a LEONARD HOUSE in Cambridge which is older in appearance than in date. Author, 1954.

An old photograph of SANDY POINT or DIRICKSON HOUSE, Worcester County, a brick homestead built before 1812 and almost unrecognizably altered. This view shows the driveway front and some of the outbuildings on the plantation. Mrs. E. A. Carey.

For forty-six years, MAYFIELD, Worcester County, was a Carey home. Destroyed by fire in May, 1955, the dwelling, even in the older "ell" behind, did not date before 1800. Below, on the BURLEY MANOR lawn in 1890, two members of the "Spinster's Club"—Virginia and Kate Hammond—pose with an admirer. A "Spinster" was a girl who had a marriage offer and had refused it.

BURLEY MANOR, Worcester County, was built in 1832-33, and is a "Hangover" Georgian home of brick covered with stucco. At the left is a china-berry tree beside the garden or back porch. Author, 1955.

SAMUEL ADAMS HOUSE, on the Lower Eastern Shore, dates from 1795, and has been recently stripped of its fine woodwork. Upstairs is a "supra-attic," lit by a single lie-on-your-stomach window. Author, 1954.

THE REWARD (1794), Caroline County, has the only early "diamond stacks" hitherto discovered in Maryland. Such stacks are medieval "hangovers" grafted upon a
dwelling of Federal Style. Author, 1953.

The old Ennalls boxwood and flower garden at EL DON, Dorchester County, has been mostly uprooted. There were originally one box circle, which was a labyrinth, and twenty-seven box squares. Author, 1954.

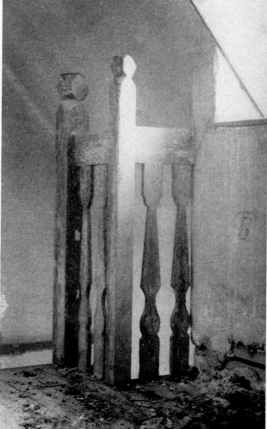

Some Maryland houses were built in what became the State of Delaware when the Mason and Dixon Line was completed in 1767. This is the MASTON HOUSE, Delaware, built in 1727, with an addition of 1733. Johnson. Right, these are splat balusters and newel posts with shaped finials on the Second Jacobean staircase found in Maryland.

The Great Room or "Hall" in the FASSIT HOUSE, Worcester County, where this writer was forbidden in 1932 to enter. Note the double-dog ears, fluted pilasters without bases, and board ceiling. E. L. Carey.

2

THE UPPER EASTERN SHORE

1. THE GHOST TOWN OF WYE

O N *Doncaster Farm*, Miles River Neck, Talbot County, lies a remnant of one of the buried towns of Maryland. This was Wye Town, located at the junction of the Miles River and the Wye River. The little settlement was created in October, 1683, at a meeting of the General Assembly of Maryland in St. Mary's City, the first capital. That Wye Town was becoming a busy place by that year is indicated by the fact that one Jonathan Hopkinson in 1683 was authorized to operate a ferry between Wye Town and St. Michaels, across the Miles River. Hopkinson was an innholder at Wye Town; and it may be surmised that if there was a hostelry at that early date, there were other buildings such as store or warehouse.

The following year, 1684, a levy was made to pay for certain workmen for laying out Wye Town. The list includes Josiah Crouch, 10 days' work, for 300 pounds of tobacco; Alexander Kinement for himself and horse, 12 days' work, for 360 pounds of tobacco; and Colonel Lloyd for his negro, 6 days, for 180 pounds of the same product.

This last reference is to Philemon Lloyd, the master of an adjoining estate, *Wye House.* He was the husband of Henrietta Maria Bennett Lloyd, that lady who was "ancestress of the Eastern Shore," and who was closely related to the

49

Bennetts, Neales, Calverts, and Brookes of Maryland, as well as to the Lees of Virginia. A pious Roman Catholic, she was responsible for the erection, before 1693, of the first chapel of that faith on the Eastern Shore. It was located at Wye Town, or Doncaster, as the settlement later became popularly known.

In connection with the founding of Wye Town there are preserved at *Wye House* two plats dated September 25, 1695, and made for Madam Henrietta Maria Lloyd by Philemon Hemsley. They show that the settlement of Wye Town was largely taken out of *Crouches Choyce*, 100 acres, and *Morgan St. Michaels*, 300 acres, lying on the east side of Chapel Cove. *Thomas Bruff's House* is shown near Town Point, across a narrows from Crouches Island, later Bruff's Island.

The Roman Catholic Chapel, called *Ye Chapple*, situated at the head of Chapel Cove and on the property called *Morgan St. Michael*, is shown in simplified sketches to be a one-storey brick building surmounted by one or two crosses. Although not shown on these drawings, an apse is believed to have been one of the significant features of the fane.

Also shown on these two plats of 1695 is the *Old Lee House*, which stood on the Miles River bank a goodly distance south of Chapel Cove. If the thumbnail sketch of it is correct, the dwelling was a little one-storey-and-loft cottage with a central door flanked by two windows and with an end chimney.

There were probably never more than a dozen buildings existing in Wye Town at one time. In truth, some of these little planned "cities" became the earliest ghost towns in the English Colonies, following the lead of St. Mary's City and Jamestown.

Of record at Wye Town, besides the inn of Jonathan Hopkinson, were the pair of stocks and a whipping post (1700) set up by Richard Bruff. In 1707, a "Platt of Donkester Town, part being 50 acres of Richard Bruff's Land" was drawn on paper. It, too, is preserved at *Wye House*. Because the original plat has been mutilated and bears handwriting which is none too clear, a tracing (p. 51) has been made which shows certain features to better advantage. In the right-hand lower corner there is written:

> Town of Donkester laid out August 4th 1707—this being that half of
> ye said Town on ye land of Richard Bruff—the Sandy beach being in-
> cluded within ye fifty acres. Platted by a Scale of 10 perches in an Inch.
> W. Turbutt.

As may be seen in the drawing, the few topographical features of the town are: the Wye River on north and west, the Chapel Cove on the south, and Town Point, marked by a Spanish oak, on the northwest. Landing Street, where there must have been a wharf, began on the north bank and ran southward, intersecting High Street, the only cross lane. Also extending southward from the north bank

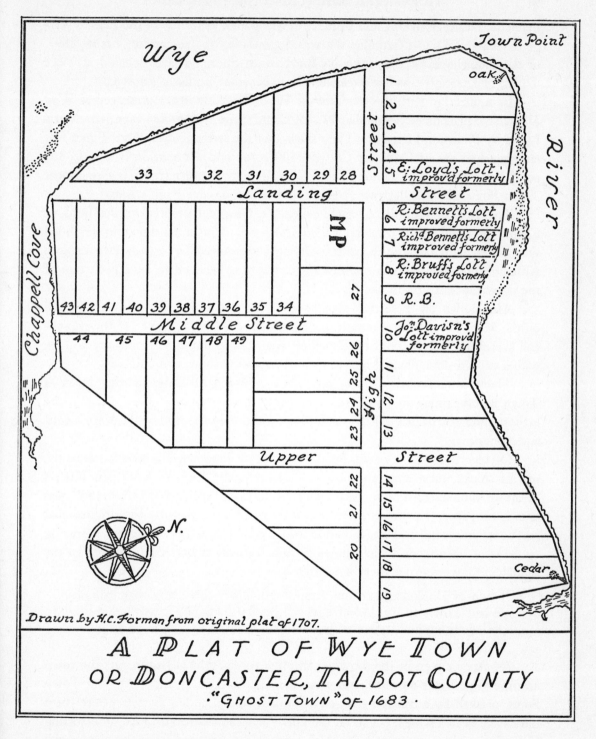

Wye

Town Point

oak I.

River

Street

33 32 31 30 29 28

Landing   Street

MP

E: Loyd's Lott
improv'd formerly

R: Bennett's Lott
improved formerly

Rich'd Bennett's Lott
improved formerly

R: Bruff's Lott
improved formerly

R. B.

Jon Davisn's
Lott improv'd
formerly

Chappell Cove

43 42 41 40 39 38 37 36 35 34

27

Middle Street

44 45 46 47 48 49

High

Street

Upper

N.

Cedar

Drawn by H.C. Forman from original plat of 1707.

A PLAT OF WYE TOWN
OR DONCASTER, TALBOT COUNTY
."GHOST TOWN" OF 1683.

parallel to Landing Street was Upper Street. The fourth and last thoroughfare was Middle Street, set out between Landing and Upper Streets, and it ran southward not from the north river bank but from High Street.

The only open space or square in the town was the Market Place, marked "M P" on the map. But since only six of the forty-nine building lots appear to have been built upon, it might be said that most of the area within the town limits was vacant. The following lots formerly had buildings upon them: Edward Lloyd's, no. 5; Richard Bennett's, nos. 6 and 7; Richard Bruff's, nos. 8 and 9; and John Davison's, no. 10. The site of the Roman Chapel is not marked. Also there are no traces of Thomas Bruff's tobacco warehouses (1707) and Bennett's store.

In naming the central lane Middle Street, the city fathers were merely copying the thoroughfare in the provincial capital, St. Mary's City, which was laid down by 1678—only five years before the founding of Wye Town. The St. Mary's middle highway had upon it some of the most important town buildings of the capital, such as Jamaica, home of Nicholas Painter; the Law Chambers of Robert Ridgely, Robert Carville, and Christopher Rousby; and the first Protestant Episcopal Church in Maryland.

There was another feature in Wye Town which has not been located: the deer park. This may have been enclosed outside the area of the town lots; or it could have been within the lots after the buildings had crumbled and great trees had grown up where the settlement once stood. The deer park was established by Edward Lloyd IV, of Wye, probably around 1765 or 1770, and is supposed to have been used by his son, Governor Edward Lloyd. It has been stated that the park was abandoned on account of the problem of fencing in the animals.[1]

Today old bricks may be found at *Doncaster Farm*, where the river bank is being washed away—a perfect setting for a small archaeological project of some historical society. Who will heed the warning that when the shore has been sufficiently eroded, there will be no physical traces of the settlement remaining?

Two relics of this general neighborhood are the little brick dwelling, built probably in the very late eighteenth century, and the great corn house, at *Wye Town Farm*, comprising 260 acres and located to the south of old Doncaster.

The corn crib, which may well be early eighteenth century, is one of the largest on the Eastern Shore, and our drawing illustrates its approximate original appearance, based on the existing remains (p. 53).

About forty feet long, the crib is divided transversely into two equal compartments by a slatted partition, having, it appears, no doorway. In other words, it was a duplex corn house. In spite of its date, it was constructed in the Hangover Medieval Style: half-timber work with vertical slats taking the place of the

[1] Tilghman, O., *History of Talbot County, Maryland*, vol. 1, p. 205.

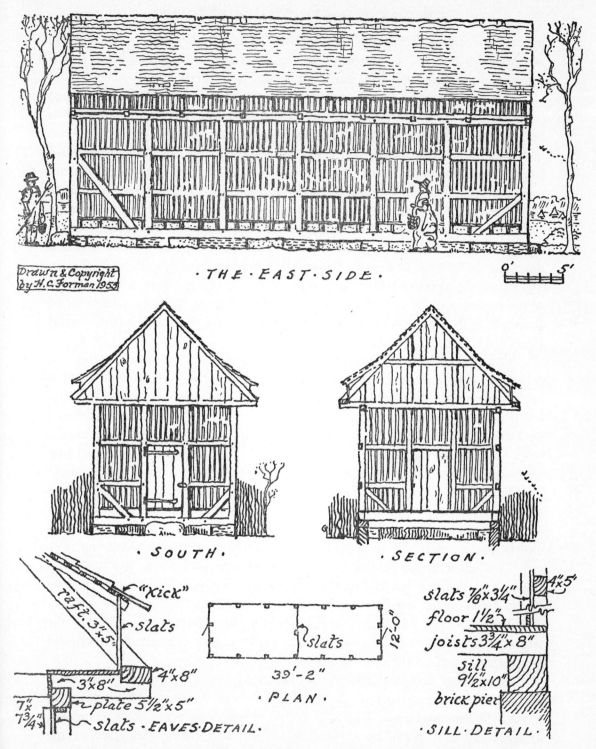

· THE · EAST · SIDE ·

Drawn & Copyright
by H.C. Forman 1955

0'   5'

· SOUTH ·

· SECTION ·

raft. 3x5"

"Kick"

slats

4"x8"

3"x8"

plate 5½"x5"

7"x
7¾"

slats · EAVES · DETAIL ·

slats

39'-2"

12'-0"

· PLAN ·

slats ⅞"x3¼"

floor 1½"

joists 3¾"x8"

4"x5'

sill
9½"x10"

brick pier

· SILL · DETAIL ·

A reconstruction by the author, of the great corn house at WYE TOWN FARM, Talbot County; an 18th-century example of medieval half-timber work, with vertical slats taking the place of wattles.

earlier wattling or basketwork employed in early England. The eaves overhung a goodly distance, twenty-one inches, and a few years after construction they were raised thirteen inches above their former level, thus forming "kicks" in the roof. In this way additional slatted ventilation was given to the upper portion of the crib. This alteration of raising the eaves gave charm to the building. On the west side a new door has been placed in position, and carries an old, wrought-iron hasp, seven and three-quarter inches in length, which probably came from one of the original doors.

The brick house at *Wye Town Farm*, built entirely in the common or American bond, is a small quaint homestead. It is shown in a very roughly-drawn plat of the farm, done by "J.M." on August 30, 1839, which is preserved at *Wye House*. The original dwelling is squarish, with a Great Room facing the water, a small dining room behind, two sloping-ceiling bedrooms upstairs, and a kitchen wing to the east. The kitchen has an open-beam ceiling and a brick floor, which was originally of dirt. The staircase, which rose at the left of the front door in the Great Room, has been removed. In this room there was no window which looked out on the water, but upstairs in the front bedchamber there was a lone dormer. Some of the interior woodwork, such as the mantels on the diagonal fireplaces in the dining room and Great Room, has been kept to a natural finish. Of interest is the outside kitchen chimney with brick steps.

On the river side, the picturesque outbuilding (p. 77), square and of wood, has two curved brackets on the front and shows nineteenth-century characteristics. Old photographs reveal a brick smoke house on the water side, the ruins of which are still visible. To the east, at a good distance, lie brick foundations of unknown size and shape. The great corn crib would appear to have served a far larger plantation house than this abode. If there was indeed a mansion, some antiquarian may yet discover its location.

About the year 1830 a letter concerning *Wye Town Farm* was written to Edward Lloyd from his "affectionate wife A Lloyd" at *Wye House*. It ran in part as follows:

> You will laugh when I tell you that Old Ned from Wye Town applied to me to go to Baltimore to get some things for his wedding—He says he is tired of living alone & means to take another wife. One of the women of Wye Town is the person. It was not convenient for him to go there, as I wanted him to catch oysters & he has supplied me very well—He is to go the next time the boat goes up.

As late as 1863 a list of Negroes taken and put in the Army by the Federal Government gives "Jim & Tom, Bill & Jim, Ike, Ennals, and Peter, all of Wye Town, the property of Edward Lloyd of Talbot County."

2. WENLOCKE CHRISTISON'S PLANTATION, *THE ENDING OF CONTROVERSIE*[1]

DOWN AT THE END of a dusty road in Talbot County and beside Golds-borough Creek, there stood until recently in an almost incredible state of ruin the seventeenth-century house closely identified with Wenlocke Christison, a man who was no less a pioneer of religious freedom in this country than John Bowne of New York or Samuel Gorton of Rhode Island. In truth, so important in the annals of Maryland is the very name of Wenlocke Christison that the Maryland Tercentenary Commission, in its brochure celebrating the founding of the Province and the establishment of religious freedom, described how Christison was persecuted in Old England and New England as well, and how he found on the Chesapeake Bay a home with the name of *The Ending of Controversie*. For all that, his house, over two hundred and fifty years old when we found it in 1935, had been allowed to become a dilapidated ruin on the brink of complete destruction, *uncared for and unknown*.

In the year 1656 there began in New England what has been generally and not improperly called the persecution of the Quakers. It was Wenlocke Christison who, for his Friends' faith, suffered twenty-seven "cruel stripes" laid on his bare body with calm deliberation in front of the standing magistrates of Plymouth, Massachusetts—standing, so that the judges, bidding the jailer lay on the whip, could the better see.

It was Wenlocke who was ejected from Plymouth prison to travel on three-pence a day in the dead of winter, the jailer having robbed him of his waistcoat and the Governor having told him that he must "pay" for his preaching. Again, it was Wenlocke who was banished from Boston for being a member of the Society of Friends, with the attendant penalty of death should he return, and who, returning, was told that, unless he renounced his faith, he should die. One can almost hear the entreaties of his companion, who stood next to him in the courtroom, whispering, "Wenlocke, thy turn is next at hanging"; but Christison, having just seen a Friend hanged, said no, he would not change his faith, nor seek to save his life. Memorable are his words on this occasion:

> for the last man that was put to death here are five come in his room, and if you have the power to take my life from me, God can raise up the same principle of life in ten of his servants and send them among you in my room, that you may have torment upon torment.

[1] Reprinted, with changes, from the *Maryland Historical Magazine*, September 1939, p. 223. See also *The Architecture of the Old South*, pp. 126, 128; figs. 157, 168, 188, 190.

Finally, it was Wenlocke who, along with two women, was stripped to the waist, tied to the tail of a cart and whipped through Boston, Roxbury, and Dedham.

It may be added here that there was nothing unusual about that whipping business. The first Quaker women to come to New England were ordered to be stripped to see if there were Devil's marks upon them, and thereafter almost every town was favored with the spectacle of girls and mothers of the Society of Friends stripped to the middle, tied to carts, and whipped without mercy.

When Wenlocke Christison found no haven in all New England—not even in Rhode Island where he stayed for a short time—and when he came to Maryland, the "land of sanctuary," it seemed entirely fitting that he should give to his plantation by the Chesapeake the name of *The Ending of Controversie*. Popular tradition would have us believe that he so named it. The brochure issued by the Maryland Tercentenary Commission stated that Christison "named his estate *The End of Controversie*." But the fact remains that his farm had previously been owned by Francis Armstrong, a planter, who had the 150 acres of *The Ending of Controversie* laid out on February 19, 1667. Armstrong likewise owned *Betty's Cove*, the site of the first Friends' meetinghouse on the Eastern Shore. He soon conveyed *The Ending of Controversie* to the Calvert County physician, Peter Sharp,

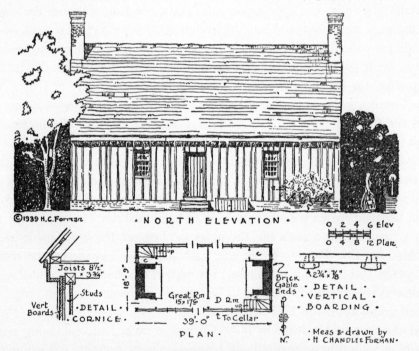

Reconstruction drawing of THE ENDING OF CONTROVERSIE (c.1670), built by Maryland's foremost pioneer of religious freedom, Wenlocke Christison.

who had a patent for it on October 10 of the same year. Not until the first of August three years later (1670) did Dr. Sharp and his wife Judith give the tract to Christison as a gift. Nevertheless, if Christison did not name it, someone else must have been buffeted, in the Old World or in the New, before finding tranquillity on this Maryland plantation of the peaceful name.

The dwelling (pp. 56, 78) ascribed to Christison was an interesting example —and a rare one, too—of a structure built with random-width boards placed vertically on the long sides of the house. This method, employed in the New England whence Christison had come, is a derivation of the oldest-known form of wooden construction in England. It may be described as a variety of the "palisade" style of building, brought to England over a thousand years ago by the Anglo-Saxons.

There is no doubt that the palisade construction at Christison's was original. The boards were very old and weathered, fitted tightly at the top under the cornice, and had wooden strips to cover the joints against the weather. Moreover, the nails were of the old, wrought-iron, square-headed type.

From an architectural standpoint the building appeared definitely to date from the seventeenth century, because of the great fireplaces, seven feet in span; the two little narrow break-neck winding staircases beside the chimneys; the vertical-board partition, with simple quarter-round moldings, separating the rooms downstairs; the cellar and foundation walls laid up in English bond; the small windows and very steep roof; the little bedrooms with sloping ceilings; and, of course, the medieval palisade walls. Indeed, the very plan is typical of the seventeenth century: brick gable ends, timber-framed sides, with two rooms downstairs and two up—like, for instance, *Clocker's Fancy* in St. Mary's City, or *Clay's Neck* in Talbot County, good examples of what we call the hall-and-parlor house.

In the Great Room (p. 73) which lay toward the east, the fireplace, large enough to take a seven-foot log, was wainscoted in simple fashion and had a large rectangular panel in the overmantel. Upstairs, the whole west end of the bedroom over the parlor was paneled in simple taste, for even strict Wenlocke Christison was influenced by prevailing hand-carving fashions. But in what condition lay that bedroom when we saw it in 1935. The arched fireplace with shelf molded in cyma curves had no back but the open air, because the brick gable had fallen out behind it. The doors to closet and staircase, as well as the central panel over the fireplace, had fallen off the house. Yet here in this room it very well may have been that Wenlocke died, his dust to be buried "in decency and in order" within a fenced area "upon the Hill" close by.

At the time of his death in 1679, Christison owned the following articles of furniture, among others: featherbeds, blankets, sheets, bolsters, pillows and pillow cases, a warming pan—possibly for the bedroom without a fireplace,—a chest of drawers, a large standing table and a round table, a large wainscot chest, a trunk marked M C (probably for his daughter Mary), rugs, and brass "twined" candlesticks. For the kitchen, which possibly lay to the west of the house, we know that he had brass kettles and brass ladles, iron pots, a bell-metal pot, a small skillet, pewter basins, and pewter dishes and porringers of various sizes. These articles, while not comprising the full furnishings of the house, indicate that *The Ending of Controversie* did not bear the stamp of poverty. In those days relatively few persons owned such luxuries as brass candlesticks which were spirally twisted.

Christison bore an honorable name in Maryland, not only among Friends but also in government circles. One of the first Quakers ever to hold public office, he was Burgess in the General Assembly, meeting in 1678 in St. Mary's City. Although he died the following year, his membership was retained until 1681, when it was noted in the records that he was a "member deceased." He left a charming widow—at least attractive enough to marry thrice. When that young woman, Elizabeth (Harwood) Christison, *née* Gary, found herself a widow for the second time after Wenlocke's death, she embarked upon two undertakings. The next property which she acquired was called *Widows Chance* (1679), and a little later (1681) she entered into bonds of holy matrimony for a third time, William Dixon, "the Glover," being the fortunate choice.

There seems little doubt that William Dixon, also called planter, lived at Christison's house after he married the widow. It is certain that Dixon owned *The Ending of Controversie* between her death in 1697 and his death in 1701. Although the tract reverted to persons called Edward Russam, John Ray, Thomas Roberts, and their wives, Isaac Dixon in 1731 possessed the whole 150 acres, so that the plantation may well be claimed as an old Dixon property.

About 1890, Wenlocke's home was mentioned as being in a "dilapidated" condition. By 1935 the brick gable end on the west had crumbled to dust, carrying with it one of the great chimneys and one of the staircases (p. 193). The floors sagged dangerously; in fact, the floor of the parlor had already departed into the yawning gulf of the cellar. The early guillotine sash had been kicked in, and the ends of the roof rafters on the south side had rotted so much that the whole roof hung tremulously suspended in air. The plaster had fallen from the crude hand-cut laths, and the doors had been stripped from their hinges. Wrecked sofas, kerosene stoves, broken planks, parts of doors, and pieces of scrap iron littered the Great Room. Such detail is presented to show what the forgetfulness of the years can do to a house. Even if this dwelling had lacked an historical background, it should have warranted preservation on the sole ground of its palisade construction in the Anglo-Saxon tradition. New England or Virginia would probably have cared for such a noted building as the heritage of the State, and possibly a Rockefeller would have bestowed on it the good fortune which the *Rolfe House*, or Smith's Fort Plantation, received.

Perhaps when Wenlocke took his last look through the little square bedroom window, the memory of his fantastic early life came back to him. It is difficult to believe that he ever forgot the time when, on trial because of his Friends' ministry, he stood before Governor Endicott of Massachusetts, who called to him, "Wast thou not banished upon pain of death?" and his own answer, calm, steady, fearless, "Yea, I was. I refuse not to die." What could you do with a man like that? What could be done with one who would sooner suffer the gallows than take off his hat? Or who, on trial for his life, tried to prove that Massachusetts had forfeited the King's Patent, at the same time turning the charges of his accusers into accusations against themselves? The Boston punishments, where the lashes of knotted ropes made holes in the body deep enough for peas to lie in, were not enough to break the spirit of this man. Christison was one of those few whose spirit is invincible, and the judges did not dare to put him to death.

The little gray cottage with the mossy roof, decaying by the sleepy river shore, was the last material monument of a man whom Maryland will long remember. Whenever we think of him, we are reminded of this Province where for many years there was an ending of controversie, and men and women could worship and live in peace together.

3. *RIGBY'S LOTT* OF THE RIGBIES

IN TALBOT COUNTY, a charming frame dwelling of "telescope" design suffered the "so-called improvements" in the year 1951, so that, although completely modernized, much of its distinctive quaintness shown in old photographs (pp. 78, 79) is now gone. The smallest section of the telescope was the kitchen portion, probably built in the middle of the eighteenth century.

The property on which *Rigby's Lott* stands is believed to have been owned by members of the Rigby or Rigbie family between 1750 and 1935. In 1797, Jonathan Rigby had the following tracts of land resurveyed: Hopkins Point, Hopkins Point Addition, Maxwell Moore, William and James, The Chest, James Lookout, and Partnership. From parts of this resurvey, *Rigby's Lott*, comprising 221⅜ acres, was formed and surveyed for Jonathan Rigby on May 18, 1797. On December 3 of the same year he was granted a patent for it.

This Jonathan Rigby was of the same family as Arthur Rigbie II, who died in 1767, and his wife, Mary LeCompte Rigbie. Arthur's father, Arthur Rigbie I, before 1677 had married Ellinor (Morris) Orem, widow of Andrew Orem, and he owned *Rigby's Discovery* (1705) and *Rigby's Folly* (1710) in Talbot County.

No connection has been traced by this writer between this Eastern Shore Rigby family and that of the Western Shore. The founder of the latter branch was James Rigby I, who came in 1659 to Maryland and settled at *Rigby*, Anne Arundel County. He was a gentleman who possessed silver tankards and silver candle cups and covers. His son of the same name married the stepdaughter of Thomas Tench, who was in 1702-04 Acting Governor of Maryland. While he was a Western Shoreman, James Rigby I owned lands in Talbot County: *Rigby's Marsh* (1663) on the Cabin branch of the Choptank River and *Cabin Neck* (1669).

But to return to this telescopic abode, *Rigby's Lott*, we find that it was owned in the late nineteenth century by James Porter Rigbie. From him the property passed through his daughter, Hester Ellen Rigbie, who married Richard Bennett Frampton, to five granddaughters: Mrs. M. C. Oxenham, Mrs. E. T. Read, Mrs. Joseph T. Bartlett, Clara Frampton, and Ida Frampton. In 1935 the place was sold out of the family.

The smallest of the three sections of this dwelling was the oldest, and this part was itself divided into three portions, built at different times. First was the one-room kitchen with flush chimney, very wide clapboards, and batten doors. Next, a small extension was built over the chimney end of the kitchen, with a quaint, squarish window with a lower sash one pane high and an upper sash two panes high. The third portion of the smallest section was an outshut on the rear or the river side, which comprised a tiny cell or aisle of narrow clapboards. This wart was probably contemporary with the second or middle portion of *Rigby's Lott*, because it overlapped the second section with a little enclosed back porch and had the same width of clapboard. The trap door in the roof and the fish-scale porch on the tallest or latest section of the telescope helped to add picturesque touches to this home, which once was of splendid composition.

It may be noted that the same kind of an outshut was placed on the rear of *Boston Cliff*, Talbot County, some time after 1729, and upon other Transitional Style dwellings in Maryland.

The dairy can be seen in both photographs (p. 79). It had a door and windows for ventilation, a brick floor, and wooden troughs once full of flowing water to keep the milk cool. The smoke house stood to the east of the dairy. Far down Maxwell Moore's Creek, at the point below *Rigby's Lott*, stood the slave quarters, now destroyed. At one time there were two graveyards on the plantation, one for white and one for colored people.

4. *PERRY HALL* OF THE GREAT BOXWOOD RECTANGLES

EVEN IN ITS PRESENT lessened grandeur, *Kirkham*, later called *Perry Hall*, in Talbot County, is still an impressive Eastern Shore plantation. The history of the place begins in the year 1659, when *Kirkham*, comprising 350 acres, was surveyed for Martin Kirk. At any rate, it was either Kirk or one of the later seventeenth-century owners who used large bricks laid in English bond to build a storey-and-loft dwelling seventeen feet and a half wide and thirty-five feet long. Part of this structure remains incorporated in the existing mansion.

About 1740, eighty-one years after Martin Kirk's survey, the property was purchased by Jacob Hindman. Now, this was the period when the early Georgian style of architecture was reaching full flower. Jacob Hindman is reputed to have built a brick habitation, which undoubtedly included on the east the earlier domicile of English bond. There are strong indications that this mansion of Hindman's was one room in thickness, and followed some of the brick foundation of the present house. But Hindman's front door must have been on the axis of the present driveway leading to the Woods Gate and the highway to Easton. There is a belief that Hindman's residence resembled the floor plan of *Ratcliffe Manor* in Talbot County, but there is no visible evidence of that theory. Proof could come only with adequate excavations and further research.

Next, *Kirkham* became the property of Jacob Hindman's son, William, whose sister, Elizabeth Hindman, married the Honorable William Perry (1746-1799) of Caroline County, a blue-eyed, light-haired gentleman with a florid complexion. After his marriage, William Perry bought *Kirkham* from his brother-in-law, moved into the Hindman mansion, and renamed the plantation *Perry Hall*. It appears that he was an energetic man, because he is reported to have extended the abode, probably toward the west, and beautified the grounds.[1] During the American Revolution he was a zealous and active patriot, and he later served as State Senator for Maryland. In 1790 he possessed fourteen slaves—the small number indicating that the great *Perry Hall* plantation had not then reached its zenith. In 1799 he died suddenly while president of the Maryland Senate.

It was during the regime of Mrs. John Rogers, *née* Maria Perry, that Kercheval, an English landscape designer, some time from 1820 to 1822 made the great garden of boxwood rectangles filled with roses and other flowers upon the broad gentle slope from the house to the Miles River. He must have designed

[1] Tilghman, O., *q.v.* vol. 1, p. 445.

this garden with its axis coinciding with the river-front door of the Hindman brick mansion, not that of the present house. Maria Rogers is said to have employed fifteen gardeners to keep the grounds trim. From her, *Perry Hall* descended to a daughter, Maria Hindman Perry Rogers, who married G. E. Muse. Their daughter was Mary Hindman Perry (Muse) Cox, who had four daughters, Alice Cox, Mary Rogers Cox who married R. P. Fletcher, Annie Amanda Cox who married James Goldsborough, and Claribel Cox who married Admiral F. H. Schofield. Mrs. Schofield is the only one of these four daughters living.

The burial of Alice Cox in 1948 at *Perry Hall* will long be remembered in the county. She had specified before her death every detail of the ceremony, and when the day came all was in readiness. Her coffin was placed upon an old farm wagon in front of the *Perry Hall* residence and pulled by two mules down past Old Ned's house, through the ancient barnyard, to the family burial plot. The coffin, with a few flowers gathered from the farm upon it, rested on pine boughs spread over the bottom of the wagon.

It must have been some time around 1822 that the main part of the Hindman brick mansion burned. At least, the moldings and mantels of the present house appear to be of the 1800-20 period. Tradition has it that the fire took place during an evening dance at the dwelling in the summertime. The place was well lit by candles, and the curtains blew in and out the open windows. The last of the guests were making their way by carriage out the long driveway toward the Woods Gate when one happened to look back. What a sight to meet the eye—and no fire engines or telephones in existence. The curtains blazed at the windows, and the smoke poured out of every crevice it could find. The guests returned to help carry the grand piano to the garden, where it lay for six months. One can imagine its tone by the time December storms appeared over *Perry Hall*. For years after the conflagration, it is said, various articles of furniture were come upon in the hidden recesses of the boxwood parterres and enclosures, where they had been placed for safety.

The main part of the dwelling was rebuilt of wood, but the chief doors on river front and approach front were placed seven feet off the main axis of driveway and garden, as may be seen on our plan (p. 65). The reason for this change in the position of the main doorways is not easily apparent. At all events, in the 1880s Victorian appendages were added to the house.

One of the reasons we have measured the garden anew and redrawn the landscape plan is that our former plan in *Early Manor and Plantation Houses of Maryland* is incomplete in several respects. Further, the garden plan of the same plantation published the same year (1934) in *Gardens of Colony and State*[2] is in

[2] Lockwood, A. G., ed., New York, 1931-34, vol. 2, p. 175.

error in several matters. Our latest drawing was made after much detective work and study in gloomy cellars, among old ruins, and under giant boxwood bushes, and probably represents the nearest approach to the original layout which can be obtained. The garden plan in *Early Manors* was correct in showing the boxwood arranged in rectangles, and that in *Gardens of Colony and State* was wrong in showing the boxwood in the shape of squares. These twenty years we have had time to ponder the question of why Alice Cox thought they were squares. It must have been that from the second-floor windows she saw the rectangles foreshortened as squares. Be that as it may, on rechecking our original measurements, we found that the average parterre or area of box was four feet longer than it was wide. They were definitely rectangles.

In design Kercheval laid out a seventy-six-foot-wide green "bowling alley"— so-called, it seems, even though the ground sloped down to the river. On either side of the alley were fifteen large rectangles of box. At the lower corners of the garden, the rectangles were curved, probably for reasons of topography. In the interstices between these thirty rectangles and the main house stood little boxwood rectangles of various sizes. In the southwest corner of the garden was a great variegated boxwood tree with a box circle around it.

Although the remaining boxwood averages about nine feet in height, it must not be forgotten that originally the flowers were the chief item in the garden; the box merely formed the border for the flowers. It is interesting, too, that of the thirty great rectangles, the two nearest the mansion house had box parterre designs of ovals within rectangles, whereas the other rectangles were plain and merely held flowers. The boxwood lane which ran down from the office building to the river was heavily lined with roses set inside the box edging. The paths between the box rectangles measure nine feet from trunk to trunk.

Bounding three sides of the garden were rosemary hedges and lilac bushes, which have mostly disappeared. There were two side gates which marked a cross axis to the main alley.

In at least three other respects the plan in *Gardens of Colony and State* needs correction: First, there were in the garden at the cross walks six *octagonal* latticed belvederes or summerhouses, covered with roses and wisteria, located approximately on our new plan. Each belvedere had four arched doorways and seats between the doorways. Second, the ice house stood in the southwest corner of the garden. Third, the well and certain outbuildings near the dwelling house were omitted, as well as the wharf at the foot of the garden.

The occupants of the 1822 era at *Perry Hall* must have been very gay. A pergola known as *The Alcove* was built across the bowling green in line with the lower edge of the garden (p. 64), and they say that dances were held there of a

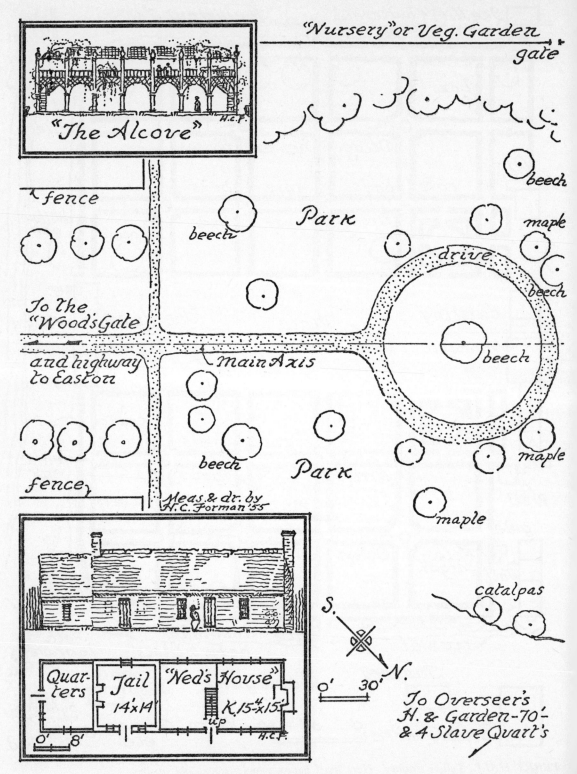

"Nursery" or Veg. Garden
gate

"The Alcove"   H.C.F.

beech

fence

beech   Park   maple

drive

beech

To the
"Wood's Gate   Main Axis   beech

and highway
to Easton   beech

Park   maple

fence

Meas. & dr. by
H.C. Forman '55   maple

catalpas

S.

N.

0'   30'

Quar-
ters   Jail   "Ned's House"
      14'x14'   K.15'x15'
0'   8'   up   H.C.F.

To Overseer's
H. & Garden - 70'
& 4 Slave Quart's

A reconstructed plan of the plantation buildings and boxwood garden at

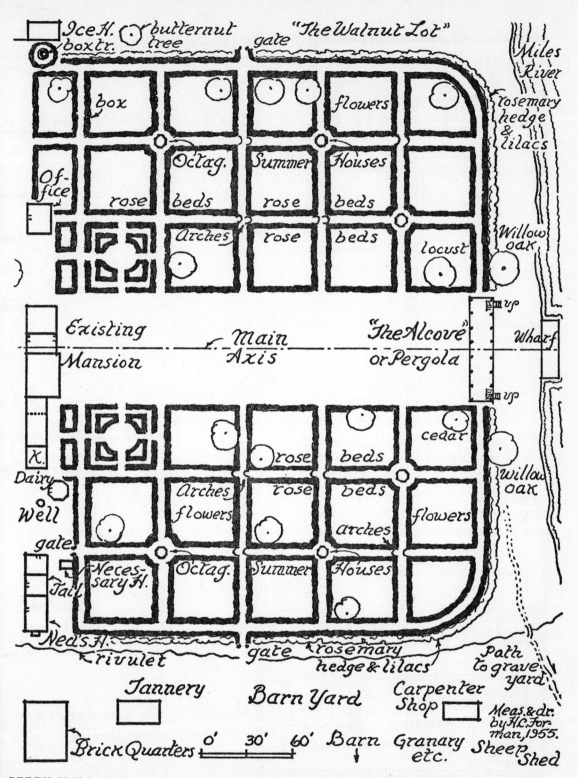

PERRY HALL, Talbot County. Here lived happy people—slaves and master.

summer evening. *The Alcove* had a series of latticed arches on columns terminating in finials and an upper deck with a balustrade around it. Access to this upper level was by a little stairway at one end of the pergola, and probably by another at the other end—in order to make a formal, balanced design. The whole structure was roofed by latticework interwoven with climbing flowers and vines. By 1878, it seems, the children then living in the mansion were forbidden to go up the pergola stairs because of the rotted condition of the upper deck. But even in that unsafe state the upper level must have been a great temptation for youngsters. By 1892 the pergola was in very bad condition, and there has been no trace of it for the last several years.

Looking from the dwelling down the broad green path, one must have seen the river twinkling with silver flashes through the vines and arches of *The Alcove*.

Maria Rogers, the lady who had the fifteen gardeners, also owned, it is told, five house servants and one hundred slaves. In order to keep such a large farm in tip-top condition she must have needed every one of them. Her father, William Perry, died without revealing to her or to anyone else where he had buried a large surplus sum of money. Accompanied by a slave or two, she went carefully around her grounds with a hazel wand, which refused to turn, thus giving no indication of the whereabouts of the treasure.

It is further related that a granddaughter of Maria Rogers went to Baltimore to consult a clairvoyant, who told her that she saw a "cellar lined with river stones," adding, "You will never find the treasure, but one of your descendants will locate it if he is attended at the time by a Negro." Those were the only words that Maria Rogers' descendant could get out of the old soothsayer. But the lady had guessed correctly that there were footing boulders under the brick cellar walls of the westernmost section of the present house. There is no doubt about them: the river stones are there.

Since then the dirt floor of the cellar has been dug in vain, even though the required attendant was present. No golden glints have come from the dark and spidery basement.

The garden at *Perry Hall* is bounded on the south by the dwelling and park, on the east by the barnyard, on the north by the Miles River, and on the west by the *Walnut Lot*. A great tree once thought to be the largest butternut tree in the United States stood back of the ice house in the *Walnut Lot*. Later it was discovered that it was a hybrid between an English walnut and a black walnut. Its nuts resembled butternuts.

Exactly aligned with the house on the driveway side there stands a row of outbuildings: on the west, forty-five feet away, is the little frame office, sixteen by twenty feet in size, where the owner of the plantation kept his accounts, per-

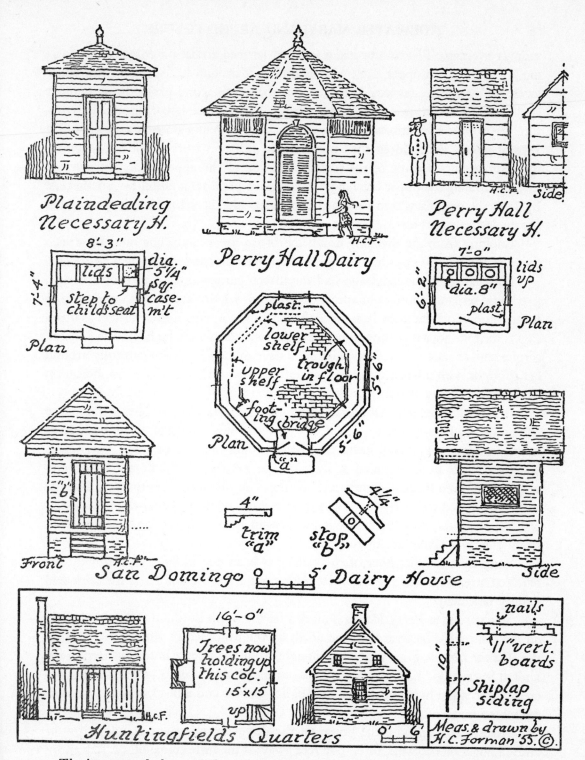

Plaindealing Necessary H.

8'-3"

7'-4"

lids   dia. 5¼" sq. case-m't

step to child's seat

Plan

Perry Hall Dairy

plast.

lower shelf

upper shelf

trough in floor

foot-ing bridge

"a"

Plan

5'-6"

5'-6"

Perry Hall Necessary H.

H.C.F.   Side.

7'-0"

6'-2"   lids up   dia. 8"   plast.

Plan

Front

"6"

4"   trim "a"

4¼"   stop "b"

Side

H.C.F.   *San Domingo   5'   Dairy House*

16'-0"

Trees now holding up this cot. 15'x15'

up

H.C.F.

Huntingfields Quarters

0'   6

10"

nails

11" vert. boards

Shiplap siding

Meas. & drawn by H.C. Forman '55. ©

The interest and charm of the early architectural styles lie largely in details, such as small outbuildings shown here, one from Southern Maryland, the others from Eastern Shore.

formed the business of making a large farm function, and held hearings on cases involving his own plantation people. The office was moved to its present position by William Perry from a point halfway down the avenue to the Woods Gate on the southwest side.

At the corner of the garden, beyond the office, stood the rectangular brick ice house, buried half underground, where children for generations, just for fun, used to slip down the roof and drop off the eaves.

On the east side of the mansion, the octagonal dairy (pp. 67, 83) and the well were set back a little from the front line, so that they would not be in the way of traffic going from the dwelling toward the farm buildings and returning. This milk house is perhaps the most charmingly designed on the whole Eastern Shore. Undoubtedly eighteenth-century, it may be contemporary with Jacob Hindman's Georgian home. It measures five and a half feet on each of its eight sides, has three arched windows with fixed slats, and one square-headed doorway with an arched transom. The doorway, it appears, had double jalousies, and the transom was also slatted. All four arches have roughly-cut keystones. On the four sides not occupied by door and windows, the upper walls have ventilation spaces covered by vertical laths. For shade, the cornice has a wide overhang, and the crowning finial has disappeared.

Inside the dairy the walls and ceiling are plastered and the floor is brick. Formerly there was a brick trough in the floor running around the eight sides of the structure, with a foot bridge over the trough at the doorway. Large gray stoneware crocks of milk and pails containing butter were kept in the water in the trough, which was piped from the bucketed well two or three times a day for the sake of coolness. Around seven sides of the inside of the dairy stands a double row of shelves, the larger shelf, seventeen inches wide, forming the lower one. An old wire mesh having nine squares to a square inch was employed at one time to screen the inside of the slatted windows.

Another outbuilding stands in line with the main house and about fifty-six feet away from it on the east. This comprises a block of three units joined together (pp. 80, 82). First is a frame room used as slave quarters in the old days and later as a chicken house. It has a batten door, one tiny window which has now been covered with siding, and a window opening with slats which were put in later. In the middle of the block is the brick jail, built of English bond like the kitchen of the main house, with footings of river boulders. This little prison measures fourteen feet square on the inside and was lit by small window openings having fixed vertical wooden bars set diagonally in the frame. There was a small inside fireplace with an opening twenty-seven inches in span. Here the malefactors were kept.

This brick jail was probably contemporary with the first brick house on the plantation and therefore seventeenth-century in date. The early owners, including William Perry, locked offenders in the jail until such time as the county authorities could take charge of them. In more recent times the prison has been used as a smoke house and as a garage. When the chicken house, on one side, and the four-room slave quarters known as *Ned's House*, on the other, were added to the jail, the exposed brick walls of the prison were covered with board studs and were weatherboarded, thus concealing the brickwork on the exterior. *Ned's House* is a typical Negro wooden quarters with two rooms downstairs—only one of which had a fireplace—and two tiny attic rooms under the eaves—true knockheads—with little lie-on-your-stomach windows for ventilation on hot summer nights. A steep, narrow, and straight staircase rises opposite the front door to the second floor.

Uncle Ned was an old darky who probably died before the Civil War began. He was talented in music, and consequently was in much demand to play his fiddle at dances and parties at *Perry Hall*, as well as other plantations in the county. The story goes that Ned came as a child from *Wye House*. Upon the occasion of a card game there, he was placed in a small chair upon a table so that all could see and hear him fiddle. He was won at cards by the owner of *Perry Hall* who took him home. Ned's son, Irving, the coach and stableman, when freed, made money at a coal-and-wood yard in Washington, D.C. He decided to spend the money on himself instead of leaving it to his children. According to his own account, Irving went on a trip to see Queen Victoria and had an audience with her. He next visited Paris and talked with one of the members of the family which owned *Perry Hall*.

Beyond *Ned's House*, at a distance of forty-five feet, stand large brick quarters, built originally of handsome Flemish bond and glazed headers and rebuilt after a fire with a changed roof line. It may be surmised that Jacob Hindman's house of about 1740 had the same wall texture as that of these quarters. Be that as it may, the quarters were large enough—thirty-nine and a half feet by twenty-nine—to serve as a habitation, having one large room downstairs with a dancing floor and a fireplace at each end. This great chamber was a recreation room and serves as a reminder that before the end of slavery life was not all labor for the black. Like the whites, he had his sociable good times. The story is told that Maria Perry Rogers used to have iced cakes baked in her kitchen and took them down in person to the dances held of an evening in the brick slave quarters. The upstairs portion of these quarters served as a dormitory for the unmarried girls.

One old Negro who had been a slave was plastering a hole in the ceiling at the dwelling house at *Perry Hall* when he was asked, "Was the colored man happier in the days before freedom than now?" His reply was: "In dem days de niggers danced and sang, and the hams hung by de hundreds. Now the niggers don' have time to fiddle and sing, and we never get a ham dat tastes like a ham."

Beyond the brick quarters, the plantation outbuildings spread out. To the east stood the great corn house, to the northeast, about seventy feet away, was the overseer's house and garden—the original dwelling having burned. Back of the overseer's house are reported to have been four slave quarters in a thorn hedge.

To the north of the brick quarters, bounding one side of the box garden, lay the barnyard containing a tannery, carpenter shop, barn, granary, sheep shed, and other structures. All these have gone except the granary. Beyond the barnyard is the family grave plot, formerly enclosed by a brick wall, access to which is obtained from the box garden by a path and footbridge over a rivulet.

There is one little outstructure which we have not hitherto mentioned. This is the eighteenth-century necessary house, located between the box garden and the chicken house. It is clapboarded with boards some fifteen inches wide, and plastered within. There are three seats with hinged lids and holes graded in size for children to grown-ups. The batten door is only five-feet-five inches high, and built of two planks totalling twenty-two inches in width. How small were the people in the eighteenth century. Our drawing of the necessary house is shown for the record and in order that it may be compared with the nineteenth-century necessary house at *Plaindealing* in Talbot County (pp. 67, 87), the only early structure remaining above ground at *Plaindealing*.

When the beloved Maria Perry Rogers died, the darkies living at *Perry Hall* composed a song about her which Uncle Ned and others must have sung for many a year:

> Old Missy Rogers died of late.
> Straight she went to Heaven's Gate,
> Where old Nick met her with a maul
> And knocked her back to Perry Hall.

5. *CROOKED INTENTION* ON SECOND CREEK

ONE OF THE original grants of land given by Charles Calvert, Lord Baltimore, to Hugh Sherwood, comprised 130 acres under the name of *Crooked Intention*. The patent was dated July 5, 1681, and the tract lay in Talbot County on the north side of the Choptank River, between that river and the St. Michael's or Miles River. Then, in 1696, fifty acres of *Crooked Intention* were sold by Hugh Sherwood to Robert Harrison I.

Sherwood died in 1710, and Harrison, who was spoken of as "of Second Creek"—now Broad Creek—made a will, dated December 22, 1717, and proved the following February 11, in which he left to his son, Robert Harrison II, *Crooked Intention* and fifty acres of land adjoining on the south called *Haphazard*, now the farm known as *San Domingo*. To his son John Harrison, also named in the will, he gave "my now dwelling plantation where I now dwell."

From the foregoing description it would appear that the home place of Robert Harrison I at the time of his death was not *Crooked Intention* but some other dwelling plantation—probably *San Domingo*. At any rate Robert II inherited *Crooked Intention* and may have built the original brick house on the place about 1717, or soon afterward, marked on our floor plan as Phase I (p. 73). To this writer the employment of common or American bond in the gable ends indicates a date later than 1717, although a feature like that taken by itself is not final proof of age.

This early structure was erected in the Medieval Style and comprised a Hall, dining room, kitchen, three knock-head bedrooms, and no cellar. The ceiling beams downstairs were exposed and beaded. The fireplace in the Great Hall or Great Room was larger than the present one and was spanned by a long oak beam. Further, the dining room had where the present fireplace stands a steep staircase, of which the original well was found by the present owners in repairing and renovating the habitation.

Toward the middle of the eighteenth century the house was changed into a Hangover Transitional dwelling of Early Cell type, marked on the plan as Phase II. This nomenclature means that the dwelling was extended at the rear, causing cat-slide roofs (p. 84) to appear over the little back cells or extensions. These changes were probably made after *c.*1730, the terminus of the Transitional Style, and are therefore Hangover.

While a cell or aisle eight and a half feet in width was added to the dining room, the spaces where such cells were tacked on Great Room and kitchen became merely extensions of those rooms. In the case of the Great Room, an interesting change was made. The gumwood plate—which is the timber on top of the wall upon which the rafters rest—was transformed into a summer beam when the rear wall was removed to make the extension. This summer beam is shown dotted in the floor plan.

In Phase II some other changes of significance were performed. The fireplace in the Great Room was made smaller. Then there were incorporated on the fireplace wall a handsome wainscoting (p. 84) with six panels in the overmantel, two of which are very long; a small china closet with curlicue shelves and glass doors; and a staircase with short balustrade and steps projecting out into the room. At the window-sill level a chair rail was put in, and a cyma cornice was installed on the fireplace side to crown the wainscoting.

The final phase of *Crooked Intention*, labeled III, was a minor one. The staircase in the dining room was demolished, and a new mantel, overmantel, and china cupboard were built in a later style—that of the American Revolutionary period of the 1780 and '90s (p. 85).

At that period the plantation was owned by Thomas Harrison, the owner of silk and cotton mills in Baltimore, and his wife, Mary (Porter) Harrison; and by their son, Samuel Harrison, "Esquire" of *Richland*—believed to be a misspelling of *Rich Neck* in Talbot County.[1] Samuel Harrison, a bachelor, is believed to have been something of a scrooge, because he pounced upon bankrupt farms and bought them at low prices. In 1805 he had *Crooked Intention*, then $150^{15}\!/_{16}$ acres and five adjoining tracts of land resurveyed as *Canton*—pronounced in the local farm idiom "*Kenton*"—and from that time until the renovation of 1948-51 the place was known as *Canton*.

During the extensive changes and alterations referred to, there were found under the first floor many pieces of china and earthernware, such as Staffordshire, Delft, and slipware. On one of the kitchen beams a pre-Revolutionary brass button came to light.

All the brickwork in the house is the common or American bond, except on the river front, where Flemish bond, with occasional glazed headers, is evident. But the unusual feature of the brickwork is revealed on the extended portion of the kitchen wing, where the common bonding has every fourth or fifth row of headers entirely glazed, in bands—somewhat like the walls of Siena Cathedral in Italy, a striped marble building.

About the main dwelling at *Crooked Plantation* stand various original outbuildings, such as corn house, dairy, smoke house, and barn (p. 85). While in a very run-down condition in 1932 when we photographed it for *Early Manor and Plantation Houses of Maryland*, *Crooked Intention* and its grounds are now kept in splendid shape.

---

[1] Gravestones: Thomas Harrison, d. Dec. 30, 1801, aged 67; Mary Harrison, consort of Thomas Harrison, b. March 5, 1737, d. June 18, 1819, in her 83rd year; Samuel Harrison, "Esquire" of "Richland," b. Apr. 7, 1777, d. June 7, 1837.

On facing page, *a reconstruction by the author of paneled walls in THE ENDING OF CONTROVERSIE, now completely destroyed: the Great Room, and the Chamber over the Parlor (later the Dining Room). Below, first-floor plan of CROOKED INTENTION, Talbot County; and floor plans of the SAMUEL ADAMS HOUSE and WINDSOR.*

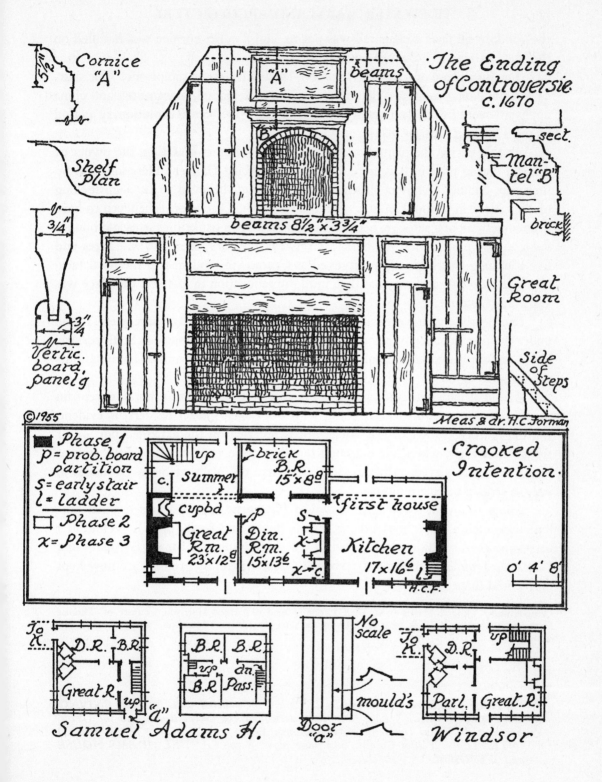

Cornice "A"

Shelf Plan

Vertic. board panel'g

$5\frac{1}{2}$"

1"

$\frac{3}{4}$"

$\frac{3}{4}$"

3"

© 1955

"A"

beams

beams $8\frac{1}{2}$" x $3\frac{3}{4}$"

The Ending of Controversie.
c. 1670

sect.

Mantel "B"

brick

Great Room

Side of Steps

Meas. & dr. H. C. Forman

Phase 1
p = prob. board partition
S = early stair
l = ladder
☐ Phase 2
x = Phase 3

up
c.
Summer
cupbd
Great Rm. 23 x 12⁸

brick
B.R. 15' x 8⁸
P
Din. Rm. 15 x 13⁶
S
x
x
c.

Crooked Intention.

first house

Kitchen 17 x 16⁶

0' 4' 8'

H.C.F.

To K.
D.R. B.R.
Great R.
up
"a"

Samuel Adams H.

B.R. B.R.
up
B.R.
dn
Pass.

No scale

mould's

Door "a"

To K.
D.R.
up
Parl. Great R.

Windsor

6. PLEASANT MISERY

BECAUSE THE SMALL brick homestead, *Mt. Misery*, in Talbot County, stands across the creek from *Mt. Pleasant*, another brick dwelling, the former used to be called by an old Negro *"Pleasant Misery,"* perhaps because such a charming residence deserved a more cheerful name.

In that low-lying country around St. Michaels, a planter, one Thomas Hethod, received a patent on October 9, 1667, for *Mt. Misery*, 100 acres lying on the north side of the Choptank River and in a creek called Second Creek—now Broad Creek. A few years later, on May 20, 1731, *Mt. Misery* and *Mt. Misery Addition*, comprising forty-one acres, were deeded by Richard Harrington and his wife, Mary, of Queen Anne's County, to William Harrison, of Talbot County, for 2000 pounds of tobacco and five pounds of current money. The above property remained in the Harrison family for about seventy-five years.

About 1805 or 1806 one Edward Covey, a slave dealer from Caroline County, obtained *Mt. Misery* at a bankrupt sale and probably built the brick house upon it. Upon his death he left the property to his daughter, Laura.

There are those who confuse *Mt. Misery* with *Haphazard*, which was never the same. *San Domingo*, of which the dairy is here illustrated (pp. 67, 87), was *Haphazard*.

Upon his first visit to *Mt. Misery* in 1934, this writer found a plain-looking brick dwelling, two storeys and attic high, with a one-storey wing and no basement. The room off the kitchen, which shows in our reconstruction sketch (p. 75), had disappeared, but its brick footings were underground. Also gone were the staircase and fireplace paneling in the Great Room. A Victorian staircase and very narrow passageway had been built in the center of the main block.

By the time of our restoration in 1954 the habitation had become a dilapidated shell: broken windows, rags, and trash on the floors, and debris everywhere. On a cold winter day with gray in the sky and wind in the trees, it was a spooky experience to try to open the front door of that abandoned and dessicated abode.

The main front of the house is laid up in Flemish bond, while the other sides are in common or American bond. Of interest are the flat arches of gauged brick and the difference in scale between the flat arches on the first and the second floor. The wing was erected simultaneously with the main block.

In the restoration drawings we called for rebuilding the half-destroyed kitchen wing and the Great Room stair and paneling. Specified were the re-erection of the attic staircase from the Hall Chamber, and the reintroduction of the dormer windows. Further, the old kitchen with arched fireplace was wainscoted to the ceiling on all sides to make a breakfast room, and a new kitchen was built into the reconstructed room off the old kitchen. Various utility spaces were incorporated in a new wooden shed or outshut on the rear or west side of the old kitchen. Unfortunately the architect's usual supervision was not permitted, so that builder's errors crept into what otherwise would have been a good reconstruction—and we now learn of a spotted roof and "builder's" stoops with soldier courses. As the French say, "*Que voulez-vous? C'est toujours comme cela.*"

Under each of the two little winding staircases are three closets for storage. The sloping paneled soffit of each stair slants at an angle in order that the upper closet door can make clearance—a naïve and rustic touch to old *Mt. Misery*. At the top of each staircase, at the bedroom floor level, are short balustrades some two feet high, with square newels and balusters and with heavy handrail.

Preliminary sketch by author for restoration of MOUNT MISERY, built c.1805-06 in Talbot County, showing west or river side. Compare p. (86).

7. THE LITTLE ROYAL *WINDSOR*—GOING, GONE

HIDDEN IN A field of high weeds and tangled vines in Queen Anne's County stands a small brick house named for the British Royal family and long forgotten. The seat was erected in the eighteenth century, probably in the 1770s or '80s, and belonged to members of the Richardson family. It is in the Hangover Transitional Style, of Late Cell type—that is, there are rear cells or aisles, and the gables are symmetrical.

The walls are built substantially of Flemish bond, and the wide brick chimneys rise flush with the gable ends. The cornice is heavily molded—a really classic affair—with Wall-of-Troy design, and at the gable ends the cornices return on themselves. Traces of the little porch with segmental or flattish barrel vault over the main entrance may be seen in the photographs (pp. 89, 90). There are evidences of delicately-molded pilasters.

The main entrance door had a transom light, and the wide jambs are paneled. This door opens directly into the Hall or Great Room, which has a handsome dentil cornice and fireplace paneling to the ceiling. In fact, all the downstairs fireplaces have mantels and overmantels, and the walls are wainscoted to the height of the window sills.

At the left-hand side of the Great Room is the parlor (p. 73), with its fireplace catercornered and its cornice heavily molded. At the rear of the Great Room is the stair passage, having a Wall-of-Troy cornice which repeats the same motif on the exterior. At the back of the parlor is the dining room with another diagonal fireplace, and an outside doorway which gave upon a kitchen wing, now gone.

Little *Windsor* is a gem of eighteenth-century architecture. Consequently it is a pity to see great holes in the roof, most of the window sash absent, partitions which have collapsed, and hand woodcarving which is neglected. When one sees the common run of ugly builder's ranch houses along our main highways today, it is to be wondered that dwellings like *Windsor*, designed by craftsmen who had high skills and artistic sense, should be allowed to deteriorate and become forgotten.

The quaint kitchen wing of the early brick dwelling at WYE TOWN FARM, Talbot County. At right, the outbuilding with curved brackets. Below, the 18th-century corn house, one of the largest in Maryland, on the same farm. Author, 1954.

*All that remained in 1935 of Wenlocke Christison's home, THE ENDING OF CON-
TROVERSIE, Talbot County, which has now disappeared. The brick gable-end had
collapsed. Below, RIGBY'S LOTT, the 18th-century dwelling of Jonathan Rigby, as
it formerly appeared. Author, 1935.*

Before the "so-called improvements" of 1951, RIGBY'S LOTT had an "outshut" on the river side and a dairy building, shown at the right. Oxenham.

A few of the original thirty boxwood rectangles, as seen from the second floor of the PERRY HALL mansion. This box averages nine feet high. Author, 1934. *Below is a view of the necessary house and the quarters-jail outbuilding.* Author, 1954.

PERRY HALL, Talbot County, from the air, showing the Miles River in the foreground, the "bowling green" and boxwood garden in front of the house, and on the left, the barnyard with brick quarters, barn, and granary. Where the driveway trees narrow was the "Woods Gate." Hollyday.

Springtime four-o-clocks on the so-called "bowling green" at PERRY HALL, Talbot County. Author, 1955. Below is the outbuilding containing "Ned's House," the chimney of which has now gone; the brick jail, weatherboarded over; and the quarters. Author, 1934.

The eighteenth-century octagonal dairy at PERRY HALL, formerly "Kirkham," Talbot County, has a jalousied door with round slatted transom with keystone. The wide cornice gave shade. The finial has disappeared. Johnston.

CROOKED INTENTION, *Talbot County, was a Medieval Style dwelling, belonging to the Harrison family. Later, the roof lines were charmingly changed. Below, the Great Room, with a glimpse of the summer beam. Author, 1955.*

The dining room mantel and glass china cupboard at CROOKED INTENTION were installed in the 1780s or 90s. Below, the timber-framed milk house, and the brick smoke house, on this plantation. Author, 1955.

The waterfront façade of MOUNT MISERY (about 1805-06), was much altered from the original before modified restoration drawings were made in 1954. Below, the dining room, with mantel stripped, and a staircase with quaint, crooked, panelled soffit. Author, 1954.

The dairy at *SAN DOMINGO, formerly HAPHAZARD, an old Harrison place, has wide eaves for shade.* Below, *the 19th-century necessary house at PLAINDEALING, Talbot County.* Author, 1954.

CUMBERLAND, where the old well was used until recently, has been unfortunately changed by the "so-called improvements." Below, LOCUST GROVE, a dwelling with a collapsing roof, has handsome pine panelling in the Great Room. Author, 1954.

WINDSOR, Queen Anne's County, was probably built in the 1770s or 80s. Below is the church at Leeds, Cecil County, showing the finely-fitting stonework characteristic of the counties bordering Pennsylvania. Chimneys, door, and shutters are not original. Author.

Clear evidence of the original front porch may be seen on the walls of WINDSOR. Note the large "Wall-of-Troy" moulding in the cornice. Author, 1948.

THE MASTON HOUSE (1727), a Maryland house in Delaware, comprising one room and loft, was added to in 1733. Note chevron design, glazed Flemish bond, and brick corbels. Johnson.

Delightfully touched with later Victorian-Gothic "icing" details, this brick mansion of the Revolutionary period is called the DAFFIN HOUSE, on Tuckahoe Creek, Caroline County. It was begun in 1774 by Charles Daffin and completed in 1783. Johnston.

An attic bedroom of the Revolutionary period in the wing at the DAFFIN HOUSE, sometimes called the THAWLEY HOUSE, in Caroline County. Here is one of the quaintest bedroom compositions in Maryland. In the deep shadow is another door. Johnston.

3

SOUTHERN MARYLAND

1 . THE *ROSE CROFT* IN OLD ST. MARY'S CITY[1]

U PON the threshold of the *Rose Croft* plantation one enters a garden where fact and fancy have long met and intermingled. One reason for this curious *mélange* is the isolation of the place, and another is the gap in the historic records. For the very seclusion of the *Rose Croft* and its bowers has caused the estate to become a thing apart in this hedgeless country, and therefore a haven of romance. The croft, as the Anglo-Saxons once called a farm, is situated in the city of St. Mary's, the oldest settlement of Maryland, at the furthest extremity of pine-bordered Mattapany Street, the first highway of this Province. It lies sequestered upon a headland carrying the bygone name of St. Inigoes Neck, and even the town, of which it is a part, seems remote.

Fancy steps in where truth can not find a way. So it was that the novelist, John Pendleton Kennedy, fell in love with the *Rose Croft* and St. Mary's a little over a hundred years ago, and in *Rob of the Bowl*[2] told of the beauteous Blanche Warden who lived with her father in the *Rose Croft*. Among the trellised gardens there, she developed a strong affection for the dashing secretary of Lord Baltimore, who on his part returned this deep devotion. It was a pretty romance; but histori-

1 Reprinted, with changes, from the *Maryland Historical Magazine*, March 1940, p. 26.
2 *Rob of the Bowl: A Legend of St. Inigoes*. Phila., 1838.

cally there is no record of a Blanche Warden having lived there. No matter. Kennedy was merely expressing the spirit of the plantation, and, besides, who can deny that a lass *like* Blanche must have dwelled there some time during the three hundred and more years of the *Rose Croft* history?

The value of Kennedy's description for the purposes of this article is primarily archaeological, for he bequeathed suggestions as to the appearance of the *Rose Croft* dwelling of the eighteenth century. It appears that there have been two houses on this site before the present modern structure. The first one was probably built in the seventeenth century, but was not known as the *Rose Croft,* which was a local designation of later date. At any rate, it was erected on that Town Land of the great Chapel Freehold known as St. Inigoes Neck and granted in 1639 to a Jesuit Priest, "Mr." Ferdinand Poulton. The other portions of this Chapel Freehold comprised St. Mary's Hill, where Poulton had a house, and the Chapel Lot, where *St. Maries Chapell,* the first English Roman Catholic church in this country, was built.

After the accidental shooting of the Jesuit priest, the Chapel Freehold passed to "Mr." Thomas Copley, the priest whose grandfather had fled to France to become knighted by a French king. Then, in 1641, Cuthbert Fenwick, the attorney of Thomas Cornwaleys, came into ownership of the tract; and it probably was during the period which followed that the first house was built with the small cellar foundation, existing, like a vault, under the present structure at the *Rose Croft* (p. 97). Indeed, it is difficult to see how the early settlers could have overlooked the placing of a building on such an important and commanding town site as that of the *Rose Croft,* where the two principal waterways, St. Mary's River and St. Inigoes Creek, join.

The cellar brickwork of the first dwelling is English statute brick laid up in English bond, characteristic of buildings of the seventeenth century in this region. The two rooms of this basement are very small, one being nine and a half feet long, and both only fifteen feet wide. Evidently the house itself was one of the smallest in the Colony and comparable to the first Leigh dwelling in St. Mary's City. Even the two rooms of little *Resurrection Manor* were three feet wider than those of this early cottage on the *Rose Croft.*

The second house,[3] of the Transitional Style, was erected to include the basement of the first. Its date of building may have been about 1706, although from the standpoint of architectural criteria the date of 1724 when Mary Van Sweringen held the premises is just as acceptable. At one time or another the Van Sweringens seem to have owned nearly every tract along the town bank of

[3] See footnote, *Maryland Historical Magazine,* March 1940, p. 27, and the writer's *Jamestown and St. Mary's,* p. 316.

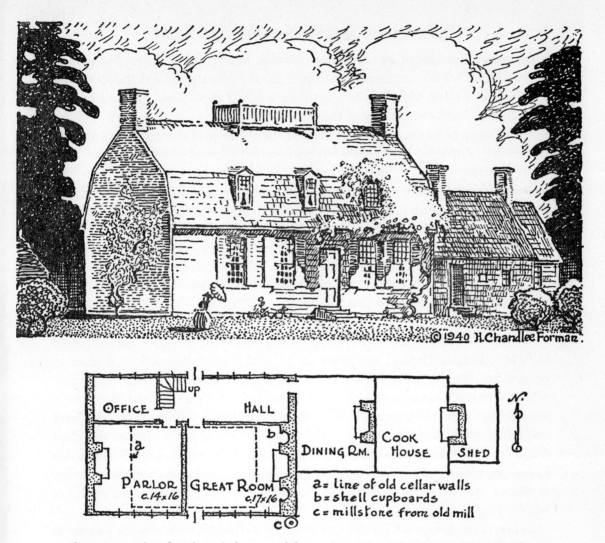

OFFICE HALL up

a

PARLOR
c.14×16

GREAT ROOM
c.17×16

DINING RM.

COOK HOUSE

SHED

b

c

a = line of old cellar walls
b = shell cupboards
c = millstone from old mill

© 1940 H. Chandlee Forman.

A reconstruction drawing of the second house (c.1706) on the ROSE CROFT plantation, within the limits of St. Mary's City. The lines of the cellar of the first dwelling are shown dotted on the plan.

St. Inigoes Creek. The father of the family went by the name of "Monsieur" Garrett Van Sweringen. He was the former Sheriff of the Dutch Colony on the Delaware, who had, it may be recalled, publicly broken his sword against his knees after the capture of his settlement by the English. In St. Mary's City, in 1672, he owned the Town House within the Fort, and when it burned he had means sufficient to rebuild it with brick. Be that as it may, Mary Van Sweringen had a charming timber-framed dwelling at the *Rose Croft*. The gable ends were brick, the long sides wood, and the roof was a gambrel. At the rear of the Great

Room and parlor were two cells or aisles as are often met with in Transitional houses. One of these was a little office, the other the stair passageway. The shell-carved cupboards in the Great Room were much like those of *Sotterly*, St. Mary's County, and the elaborate wainscot was painted blue.

Although he made no note of these cupboards, Kennedy did mention the profusion of chiseled woodwork. On the east side of the abode lay a wing containing the dining room, cook house, and shed. On the top of the roof was a small balcony or platform, constructed as an observatory, from which vessels approaching the port of St. Mary's might be described through the telescope.

About the *Rose Croft* homestead clustered a group of single-storeyed outhouses such as: the brick chapel, the smoke house, and the log slave quarters. Kennedy recorded that one of these various outbuildings was appropriated at one time by the "Collector" for his business office and could still be seen, a deserted ruin with decaying bookshelves. The "Collector" was evidently a reference to a revenue officer, who as a matter of history resided at the *Rose Croft* in 1776, and whose name was Daniel Wolstenholme. With the entrance of this man upon the scene we reach the heart of our story.

When Wolstenholme came to the *Rose Croft*, he had already performed good services for Maryland. From 1754 to 1757 he was Agent in the Supply Bill for his Majesty's Service, and helped to support the ranging parties upon the western frontier of Maryland. In the records there is an item of eighty blankets which he supplied the rangers. As an Annapolis merchant he outfitted sloops to carry provisions to military forces in South Carolina. He also served as Clerk in Chancery, and signed in 1765 the Resolutions to repeal the Stamp Act.

The outbreak of the American Revolutionary War saw him performing the duties of the Collector of His Majesty's Customs in the North Potomac District. In this capacity he no doubt used the captain's walk on the roof of the *Rose Croft* to espy approaching vessels for interception. Nevertheless, his task must not have been easy at this time, for he was a revenue officer loyal to the King and to Royal Governor Eden of Maryland. On the excuse of ill health Wolstenholme succeeded in obtaining a passport with which to embark for England. On July 20, 1776, Eden wrote him at the *Rose Croft* that the Governor's ship was at his service for the journey. The St. Mary's Committee at Leonardtown unanimously approved a resolution that Wolstenholme be allowed to depart for Great Britain. Everything pointed to a successful embarkation.

Meanwhile various letters about the Collector were being sent back and forth. Major Thomas Price wrote the Council of Safety that he thought it advisable not to suffer the Collector to leave the Province; but Colonel Richard Barnes wrote that he thought Wolstenholme should be permitted to leave, especially since that gentleman was a man of honor and for several years had been anxious to go to England. Barnes wrote:

> Upon demanding of him that he would say nothing to the prejudice of the Province, he answered that he defied his worst enemy to say that he had ever done or said anything inimical or that had a tendency that way, but that he would not be bound by anything, but that the same principle which had ever been the rule of his actions, would govern his future conduct.

While waiting at the *Rose Croft* to depart, Wolstenholme had plenty of worries. American troops and officers were stationed in his house, and he was virtually a prisoner. Moreover, on July 17, 1776, a British warship covered the *Rose Croft* dwelling with her guns. Wolstenholme immediately complained to the Americans that his house and family were in danger, because the British captain did not know who was the proprietor of the plantation.

In any angry tone Wolstenholme wrote Colonel Barnes:

> I am far from disputing the General's authority [General John Dent of the Maryland forces] to receive or not to receive the flag [of truce], but I do deny that the military power hath any right to control that of the civil. If it has, the people of this province are as complete slaves as any in Turkey.

Unfortunately for Wolstenholme, when the British did send a ship's boat with a flag of truce to pick him up, the Americans prevented his leaving. As luck would have it, the ship's boat belonged not to Governor Eden's vessel but to that of one Captain Montague, an officer who had already broken a truce off Annapolis and therefore was *persona non grata*. The Council of Safety then ordered that no one could leave the Province. Times had changed, it said, since the granting of Wolstenholme's passport, and British men-of-war were openly invading the Province. The Collector thereupon sent word to Eden that he had been twice stopped from embarking by the commanding officer at St. George's Fort, and that "no sinister events whatsoever shall ever shake those principles of honour becoming an officer in his Majesty's service."

After these stirring weeks at the *Rose Croft* plantation, the customary quiet must have surged softly backward over the gardens and house. At the close of the eighteenth century the boxwood and the rose vines were no doubt well on the way to maturity. Into this tranquil scene stepped George Campbell and his wife, Ann Biscoe. But a tragic spirit came to hover over the gardens, for these new owners were cut off from life in the bloom of their youth. The gravestones in the field at the *Rose Croft* state that George Campbell departed this life at the age of thirty-two on May 11, 1806, and that his wife Ann did likewise at the age of thirty on March 21, 1807. Their son, named for the King's Collector, was Daniel Wolstenholme Campbell, who became a warden of William and Mary Parish.

George Campbell appears to have been a lively young man. In 1799, at the age of twenty-five, he was involved in a graveyard prank in St. Mary's City, and this event is fact, not fiction. On August 5 of that year, John Mackall, Jr., laid before the vestry of William and Mary Parish:

> a complaint against James Biscoe, George W. Campbell, Alexander Mc-Williams and Joseph Thomas for breaking & entering a vault in St Mary's Church Yard & exposing to publick view the corps taken therefrom on the 27th day of July last. The Vestry on taking the same under consideration are unanimously of the opinion that the act was illegal, indecent and immoral, & that the perpetration thereof must mean the censure of this body.

Further details of this prank are given in a letter to his mother by McWilliams, one of the perpetrators. He wrote that after four hours of difficult work a leaden coffin, marked with the letters A L, was uncovered and found to contain the mummy of a lady who had turned as black as the blackest Negro. The monogram, he thought, belonged to the wife of Sir Lionel Copley, first royal governor of Maryland.

Different versions of the graveyard prank are given in Stanley's *Pilate and Herod* (1853), where the men were under the influence of liquor and the corpse was that of Lady Ann Calvert, and in Ridgely's *Old Brick Churches of Maryland* (1894), where the dignitary and his wife crumbled to dust. But the factual account is related in the Vestry Proceedings of William and Mary Parish.

It was in the decade of the 1860s that the main part of the *Rose Croft* house was altered by the addition of a full second storey and attic. As may be seen in the photograph (p. 135), porches with Victorian jigsaw brackets and a central gable with bull's eye were embodied in the revised structure. With these changes the *Rose Croft* declined into the vale of years, and during the ownership of an Englishman about the year 1900 finally met that fate meted out to so much of our early architecture—destruction by fire.

Although the gambrel-roofed house crowned by the captain's eyrie has disappeared, much of the original garden still remains. The odor of boxwood permeates the air, and, beating against the headland, the plashing tide makes faint murmurs in the bowers. The low, flower-spangled hedges of thorn, the clumps of rose trees, the rustic seats along the walks, the parterres, latticed sheds, and vine-clad gateways are no longer all there, but enough survives to make interesting a visit to this *Rose Croft* where history and romance meet.

2. THE ST. MARY'S CITY *CASTLE*, PREDECESSOR OF THE WILLIAMSBURG *PALACE*[1]

THE RECENT DISCOVERY of the ruins of the *Governor's Castle*, first known as *St. Peter's*, lying within Maryland's olden capital of St. Mary's, invites a revision of the known chronology of early American architecture. Heretofore, teachers and students of art have talked in general terms about an early "farmhouse" or "cottage" colonial type of building commonly existing in the seventeenth century in the American Colonies. This conception should be altered in view of what is now known about the *Governor's Castle*, here described at length for the first time.

By means of a research grant awarded in 1940 by the American Council of Learned Societies, Washington, the writer used the experience gained while directing excavations of Jamestown foundations for the government to conduct explorations at the site of the *Governor's Castle*, a place in St. Mary's City long known to tradition. Until digging was commenced on September 6, 1940, no one in our own generation knew what had been the size, shape, or orientation of this vast pile, built originally far back from the steep river bluffs. There was nothing above ground to convey a single indication of what kind of structure the *Castle* had been. By means of exploratory trenches in the ground, the brick foundation was finally located in the middle of a tobacco field. After the main outlines of the cellar had been uncovered, it was found that more than 11,500 cubic feet of dirt and debris lay inside the basement. The writer's reconstruction drawings (pp. 102, 103) are based fundamentally upon a study of this cellar and of old descriptions of the building. From this study it is now possible to visualize with some degree of certainty the original appearance of the mansion. These drawings are, of course, subject to further discoveries.

It is a rare thing to find in the period of the early settlements a building which was equally significant from both an historic and an architectural standpoint. In the first place, it should be recognized that the *Castle* was the most historic house of early Maryland, since it served as the home of Lord Baltimore, the Lord Proprietor of that Province, as well as the domicile of the first Royal Governors. Besides, the *Castle* possessed, as far as is known, the largest floor area of any residence built by Englishmen on the shores of the New World by the end of 1639. It was the largest dwelling of its time in the Colonies. The only larger, contemporary structure known was Harvard College, which was built of wood and

[1] Reprinted, with changes, from the *William and Mary College Quarterly*, April 1942. Further description is given in *The Architecture of the Old South*, pp. 108-112.

Side of "Governor's Castle"

Author's reconstruction drawings of THE GOVERNOR'S CASTLE, most historic house in early Maryland. The Jacobean floor plan, with a room of the same size in each corner, was unique in this country.

A Reconstruction of the First Floor Plan of The Governor's Castle (c.1639) St. Mary's City

Gate

Gate

20'x11'

25'x 20'

25'x 20'

20'x 11'

Brick Wall

Brick Wall

Courtyard

Conjectural: openings & stairs.

Meas. & dr. by H.C.Forman'42

N.

Main Gate

0'   24'

completed some five years after the *Castle*. In the third place, the floor plan of the *Castle* is unique. There is no other floor scheme of the period in this country even remotely resembling it. Finally, because of certain similarities between them, the *Governor's Castle* in its external aspect seems to have set the style approximately —or perhaps formed the prototype—of the great *Governor's Palace* in Williamsburg, which was completed between 1713 and 1720, some seventy-four years later.

The story of the *Castle* begins more than three centuries ago, when Sir John Harvey was constructing at Jamestown what was to be the first State House in

THE GOVERNOR'S CASTLE or ST. PETER'S (1639), St. Mary's City, as reconstructed by author after excavations. The largest house of its time in the Colonies, once Lord Baltimore's home.

Virginia, and the Second Lord Baltimore, Cecil Calvert, was founding the Colony of Maryland. Among the outstanding settlers who came to St. Mary's City in Maryland was one Thomas Cornwaleys, whose relative of the same name surrendered at Yorktown about a century and a half later. At all events, Thomas was the premier statesman of Maryland, and he it was who wrote that security of conscience was the first condition which he expected from the government of that Province. In April, 1638, four years after the first settling of St. Mary's City, he advised that he was constructing "of A house toe put my head in, of sawn Timber framed A story and half hygh. . . ." By May, 1640—two years later—he was using another abode, the *"Brick house"* on St. Peter's Freehold, St. Mary's City, a structure which was then described as having been "lately set up." Now the *"Brick house"* was definitely the mansion called *St. Peter's*, or the *Governor's Castle*, the subject of this sketch. Thus it appears that the *Castle* was completed either in the latter part of 1639, or in the first four months of 1640, and that it was begun in late 1638, because it must have taken more than a year to build.

When Thomas Cornwaleys in 1659 sailed home to England, never to return, the *Castle* probably stood vacant in St. Peter's field until in 1664 Chancellor Philip Calvert, that uncle of the Lord Proprietary for whom William Penn had a word of praise, obtained a new patent for the property. The Proprietary regime at the *Castle* lasted exactly twenty years. During the tenure of the Chancellor, the spacious pile was spoken of as *The Chancelor's House at St. Peter's*. In 1682, he died "seized of St. Peter's without issue," and the estate descended to his heir-at-law and nephew, Charles Calvert, that colorful Third Baron of Baltimore who resided in Maryland with all the state of a king in a small kingdom. Like Cornwaleys, the Third Baron departed for England (1684), never to return. Again the dwelling must have stood untenanted on its green sward.

While he served as first Royal Governor of Maryland (1691-93), Sir Lionel Copley is believed to have resided at the *Castle;* and this belief is further strengthened by a reference in 1692 citing "the Governor's house at St. Peter's." Sir Lionel was buried in 1693 near the present ivy-covered Trinity Church in St. Mary's, and the very same year Sir Edmund Andros "descended" upon the town and proclaimed himself governor. He, too, seems to have been a transient dweller at the *Castle* or *Governor's House* where he kept a hoard of explosives. In the language of the old record, there were "left in the Governors house 18 whole Barrlls in [gun] powder."

When he later became Governor of Virginia, Sir Edmund Andros was criticized for his activities in Maryland, such as stealing money from the Treasury in St. Mary's City. In connection with his high-handed seizure of that Province, his enemies brought out a skeleton from his closet by telling a story—not a pretty tale by any means—about an event which took place in the *Governor's Castle*. It developed that certain American Indians were so "mad" with Andros' "obscure and unsincere way of talking and acting, that they perfectly hate[d] him."

> "One of the Indian Kings in the year 1693," so ran the tale, "came to wait upon him at his house; and after a long conversation with him whereat the Indian appeared to be exceeding uneasy, he [the Indian] came into the Governour's kitchen, and finding a Case-knife upon the dresser, immediately cut his own throat therewith, and dyed.

This event happened in 1693, and it would seem bad enough not to be surpassed by any other. Nevertheless, something worse took place the following year at the *Castle*. This bulky pile of brick, the proud home of the Baltimores and of the Royal Governors, was blown skyward by the explosion of seventeen kegs of gunpowder stored presumably in the great basement. There is no record who the villains were in this case.

Tradition has it that Sir Francis Nicholson, from 1694 until 1698 Royal Gov-

ernor of Maryland and afterward head of the Virginia Colony and founder of
Williamsburg, lived at the *Castle* in St. Mary's, which continued to be known as
the *Governor's House*. On June 26, 1694, an accounting of the "Armes and am-
munition at St Maries" was made, and 192 muskets, accompanied by seventeen
gunpowder barrels, were found at the *Castle*.

It does not require too great a stretch of imagination to reason why the *Castle*
was blown up in the first week of October, 1694. One has only to take into con-
sideration the state of high feeling which at that time was coursing through St.
Mary's City. It was Francis Nicholson who in this very month of October forced
a "must" bill through the Maryland legislature to remove the seat of provincial
government from St. Mary's and to make Annapolis the new capital. The oppo-
sition which this act encountered was assuredly strong enough to set a spark to
the *Castle*. Nicholson was not only transposing a capital, but also striking the
death blow to the old Catholic, Proprietary regime which St. Mary's City repre-
sented. Where he was at the time of the explosion is not known, but he lived
long enough to name two streets in Williamsburg after himself.

On October 9, 1694, there was drawn up "A List of the Armes which were
blowne up in the Chancelor's house at St. Maries"—for even by that time men
could not forget the Chancellor who had once owned the *Castle*. The inspection
revealed that thirty-eight musket barrels were among the "broken Armes found
after the blowing up of the Chancelor's house." The following year there was
another reference to the "Countreys powder . . . burnt in the Great house at St
Maryes."

After an active life of fifty-five years, the *Governor's Castle* seems to have
moved into the realm of forgotten sites, its stalwart walls gradually crumbling for
another century and a half. A long time elapsed during which we know exactly
nothing about this historic dwelling. It was not until about 1836 that John Pendleton Kennedy, the novelist, visited St. Mary's City, and in his *Rob of the Bowl* first
gave the name *"Governor's Castle"* to the building. The appellation was, he
thought, colloquial, and is believed to have originated during the occupancy of
the Royal Governors.

"The ample dwelling-house," he wrote, "was a massive building of dark
brick, two stories in height, and penetrated by narrow windows."

It is perfectly true that in 1639 narrow windows formed the usual embellish-
ments of buildings, and the leaded glass found by the writer in the *Castle* basement
suggests the usual casements of that period. Furthermore, Kennedy described the
roof as having been "capped by a wooden balustraded parapet, terminating, at
each extremity, in a scroll like the head of a violin, and in the middle, sustaining
an entablature that rose to a summit on which was mounted a weathercock." This

is a very detailed description and must have had some truth in it if it was not wholly correct. The entablature to which he refers was probably a kind of cupola with moldings.

According to Bryant and Gay, whose *Popular History of the United States* was published in 1878, the *Castle* possessed "two stout chimneys about the middle of the house." Unlike those of the *Palace* in Williamsburg which flanked the balustraded parapet on either side, the two chimneys of the *Castle* must have risen —at least, so the exigencies of the floor plan required—at the front and the back of the parapet, in such a manner that a traveler approaching the main entrance would be unable to see the rear chimney because of the one in front.

To search for antecedents of the *Castle* floor plan, one has to go back to Jacobean styles of architecture in England. The *Castle* is exactly square, fifty-four feet on a side, with a room of the same size in each of the four corners. Such square-shaped blocks were built in England in the time of James I and are exemplified by *Bolsover Castle*, Derbyshire (1613), or *Clegg Hall*, Lancashire (1620). Nevertheless, when the great back-to-back fireplaces in the exact middle of the *Governor's Castle* are noted, it is clear that here is no Jacobean feature, but a pure medieval characteristic. The *Castle* represents a Jacobean graft on the medieval tree.

The mansion which formed the nearest competitor to the *Castle* in size was *The Green Spring*, Sir William Berkeley's home near Jamestown, Virginia, built not earlier than 1642 and hence postdating the great pile in St. Mary's City. Since the *Castle* had a floor area of 2,934 square feet, *The Green Spring* was not "the first great house of the American Colonies," as claimed by Waterman and Barrows in their *Domestic Colonial Architecture of Tidewater Virginia* (1932), because that contained only 2,886 square feet, including the small wing at the rear. Further, *The Green Spring* did not have as many rooms as the *Castle*.

On both floors and basement of the *Castle* the back-to-back fireplaces, each measuring some ten feet within the span, heated chambers twenty-five feet long by twenty wide (p. 102). Also, the corner rooms were no mere alcoves, for each measured twenty feet long by eleven wide—just about the size of the average living room of today—and had fireplaces large enough for six-foot logs. At least, these dimensions are what the excavation indicated. In one of the corner rooms of the cellar was probably stored the gunpowder for what may be called "the gunpowder plot of 1694." In addition to all this space the *Castle* contained front and rear passageways ten feet wide which formed little rooms in themselves. It is possible that a staircase lay in one or both of these passageways next to the central chimney stack. Even in the large houses of the Colonies in this period the small winding staircase was usually employed.

Bryant and Gay were almost correct in their depiction (1878) of the "great cellar paved with square red tiles." As a matter of fact, if the two basement areas under the passageways be considered as rooms, then four rooms were floored with eight-by-eight-inch clay tiles, one inch thick, with chamfered edges, and the other four rooms were paved with nine-inch brick. The entire flooring was laid on a soft mud-mortar bed over white sand.

Charred thresholds in the cellar doorways bespeak the great combustion of 1694; but unfortunately much evidence concerning walls and paving has been destroyed in subsequent years. At one or more periods the *Castle* was turned into a quarry, and entire masonry walls were carted away. The Roman Forum, it may be remembered, suffered a like fate.

Kennedy may have been in error in declaring that the *Castle* had an "arched brick porch which shaded the great hall door," and a "series of arcades, corridors and vestibules" which "served to bring into line a range of auxiliary or subordinate buildings," such as private chapel and banqueting hall. At least, insofar as the recent excavations disclosed, there are no traces in the ground of dependencies attached to the great square basement. Nevertheless he was wholly correct when he described the "grassy court" shut in by a "sweep of wall" in front of this building. "Admission," he declared, "was gained through a heavy iron gate swung between square, stuccoed pillars, each of which was surmounted by a couchant lion carved in stone." No lions have yet come to light, but the brick footings of the courtyard enclosing wall and of the main gateway still survive solid just beneath the topsoil. The portal was ten feet wide—large enough for a coach and four—and lay exactly opposite the principal entrance door of the *Castle*.

At the risk of becoming very technical, we itemize some of the important artifacts found in the *Castle* excavations. There were several fragments of quarrels or diamond panes, $\frac{3}{32}$ of an inch and $\frac{1}{16}$ of an inch thick, indicating the use of leaded casement windows; a delicate and narrow piece of lead stripping or calme; part of a thirteen-inch H-hinge; a strap hinge with spear-shaped termination; shingle or plain tiles with the customary pair of small holes at one end.

How much influence did the design of the *Governor's Castle* exert on that of the *Governor's Palace* in Williamsburg, only seventy miles away as the crow flies? The resemblances between these dwellings of the Royal Governors are too striking to overlook. There is good reason to believe that the earlier played a kind of godfather to the later edifice, the *Palace*, built approximately seventy-four years afterward. Both brick buildings had the steep, hipped roof, the balustraded parapet, the cupola, the two stout chimneys projecting from about the middle of the house. Both were two storeys high and contained a large cellar. The *Palace* in Williamsburg had the same depth of fifty-four feet as that of the *Castle* but was six feet longer in its main façade. Therefore, in the matter of comparative size, there was not a great difference between *Castle* and *Palace*—certainly not much when the seventy-four-year interval is taken into account. Moreover, both dwellings possessed grassy forecourts with enclosing walls and wide gateways.

With due allowance for the difference in architectural styles, which in 1639 were predominantly Medieval and in 1713 classical Georgian, it does not seem unreasonable to call attention to the hypothesis that in exterior semblance the *Governor's Castle* in St. Mary's City was the prototype of the *Governor's Palace* in Williamsburg.

How this relationship came about may perhaps be explained historically. Both Andros and Nicholson were familiar with the *Castle* in St. Mary's; each served as both Governor of Maryland and Governor of Virginia. In truth, Nicholson had good reason to be familiar with the *Castle*. When he laid out the city of Williamsburg in 1699—only five years after the explosion of the *Castle*—he could not have forgotten that picture. He was not recalled from Virginia to England until 1705, the very year in which the *Palace* in Williamsburg was ordered to be erected.

In conclusion, it may be stated that the American aesthetic tradition, which, particularly in architecture, is most permanently established, is now enriched by our knowledge of the *Governor's Castle* in old St. Mary's City.

3. UNRAVELING THE ENIGMA OF
WOLSELEY MANOR

THE MANOR OF Wolseley comprised 1900 acres on the east side of the north branch of the St. Mary's River, near the Indian Bridge, and was laid out on August 18, 1664, for Chancelor Philip Calvert, the owner of the *Governor's Castle* in St. Mary's City. The reason given for this manor grant was that he "hath surrendered unto us his Manors of Morton and Swale." In naming this land, Philip evidently honored his first wife, Anne Wolseley, daughter of Sir Thomas Wolseley of Wolseley, England. His other manor of the same name, located in Talbot County, Eastern Shore, was also named for Anne. In later years, Charles Calvert, Third Lord Baltimore, seems to have been the owner, according to the Rent Roll of 1705, of the Wolseley Manor on the St. Mary's River.

In spite of what has been written about the manor house being extant on Wolseley Manor, no trace of the original manor building has ever been found.[1]

[1] *Maryland Historical Magazine*, December 1938, p. 330; *Jamestown and St. Mary's*, p. 317.

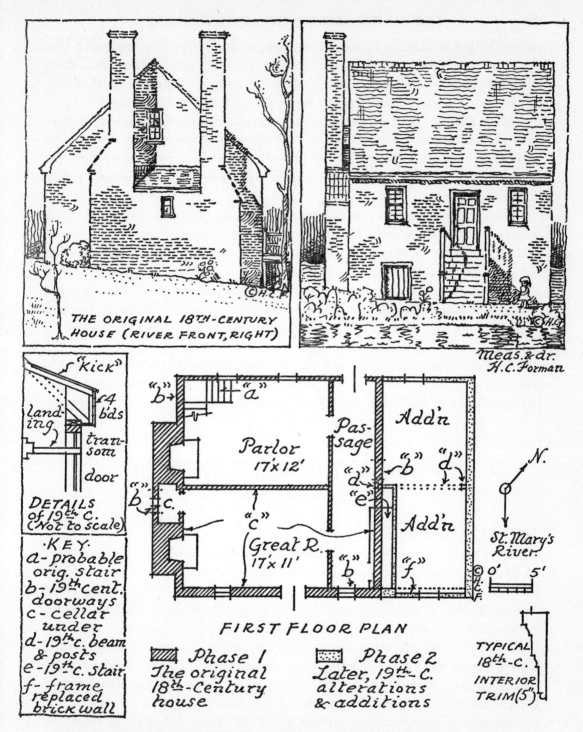

THE ORIGINAL 18TH-CENTURY
HOUSE (RIVER FRONT, RIGHT)

©H.C.F

Meas.& dr.
H.C. Forman

"Kick"

landing

4 bds

transom

door

DETAILS
of 19th C.
(Not to scale)

·KEY·
a- probable
orig. stair
b- 19th cent.
doorways
c- cellar
under
d- 19th c. beam
& posts
e- 19th c. stair
f- frame
replaced
brick wall

"b"
"a"

Parlor
17' x 12'

Pas-
sage

Add'n

"b" "d"

"b" "c.

"d"

"e"

"c"

Great R.
17' x 11'

Add'n

"b"

"f"

N.

St. Mary's
River.

0'   5'
©H.C.F

FIRST FLOOR PLAN

▨ Phase 1
The original
18th-Century
house

▦ Phase 2
Later, 19th- C.
alterations
& additions

TYPICAL
18th- C.
INTERIOR
TRIM (5")

In St. Mary's County, WOLSELEY MANOR, as it is called in the neighborhood, presented a hard nut to crack. These reconstruction drawings are submitted by the author
after many hours of study.

The house known as *Wolseley Manor* or the *J. J. Allston House*, herewith drawn, measured, and photographed (pp. 109, 136), is not Philip Calvert's dwelling. The oldest part of it above ground dates no earlier than the eighteenth century and, besides, the ruin stands on the west side, not the east side, of the north branch of the St. Mary's River.

There is no doubt that the little habitation is a mix-up as regards chronology. After several visits, the writer believes that he has found the solution to what man made of the structure over the years. One of the puzzles was why the original downstairs passageway was so narrow that there was scarcely room for a small stair. The logical place for a staircase to fit was in the chimney end of the parlor; consequently we have conjecturally drawn it thus (p. 109).

Now, to get down to brass tacks with the chronology: Phase I, the original eighteenth-century dwelling, represents a Late Cell type of structure of Transitional Style—that is, the rear cell or aisle had grown large and the gable end had become symmetrical. Three of the outside walls are brick, the rear wall frame. A typical St. Mary's County brick chimney pent between chimneys projects from the west gable, and it may have had a tiny window, trace of which has been removed. A stone cellar ran under the Great Room on the front and extended under the forepart of the passageway, marked "c" on the drawing.

The nineteenth-century owners made hash out of this dwelling, but it became even more picturesque than before. In Phase II, some of the openings on the front façade were changed around; a brick-and-frame addition was added to the east gable; the downstairs passageway was bulged out to receive a new stairway; and three doorways—one upstairs and two down—were punched in the west or chimney-pent gable wall, leading to an ungainly addition on the west, which for lack of space we have omitted from the floor plan.

By the injection of a new stairway into this snuggery, the owners were confronted with lack of head room when they built a stair landing across the transom bar of the front doorway. In fact, the transom window coincided with the level of the landing floor. There was not even room for a midget to walk under the roof rafters to gain the second floor. As a result of this problem the eaves were raised to form a "kick" on the roof, as may be seen in one of the inserts on the drawing. The raising of the roof did not form a true jetty, or overhanging storey, because the floor joists were not extended outward. The new stairway, which bulged out the front passageway, has plain balusters, set on the diagonal, and a square newel post, rounded and chamfered at the top.

The entire upstairs storey, its partitions, roof, and dormers were also done over at this time—all the trim and woodwork being nineteenth-century. The quaint chimney pent was entirely covered, its small roof being ripped off to form a deck over which to gain access to the second storey of the west addition.

The brickwork of the river front of the original house and of the east addition was poorly constructed, because afterward at various intervals portions of the wall cracked, tumbled, or threatened to tumble. In recent years cement has been copiously used to strengthen the lower portion. To confuse matters for the archaeological detective, the largest part of the front wall of the east addition collapsed altogether, leaving jagged brick edges; and a section of frame wall was inserted, inadvertently making the river front more picturesque than ever.

It has never been discovered why three of the cellar walls are of stone boulders, the fourth wall, facing the river, being of brick and not even bonded with the stone walls. Probably no one will ever know if the stone cellar antedated the original eighteenth-century building.

One of the curious features of the river front was the two windows with sash having the panes set horizontally instead of vertically. Perhaps this is an example of "Carpenter Colonial" or of Victorian eccentricity. At any rate, on the chance that they are the former, we have shown them horizontally in the reconstruction.

4. THE *FRANK SMITH PLACE* AND THE GREAT VINE

IN 1953 THE FARMER-OWNER of the *Frank Smith House*, St. Mary's County, gave notice that he planned to make a tremendous bonfire of the whole dwelling. It was to be in the nature of one of the ancient funeral pyres. By this writing, two years later, the act has no doubt been accomplished and the little ruined seat has gone up in smoke. If so, no longer will the cows wander at will through the downstairs floor.

The great vine, shown in an incipient stage of development in our two photographs of 1938 (pp. 137, 138), had by 1953 grown so large that it supported more than a quarter of the whole dwelling. In fact, by that time half of what remained of the roof sagged in space, buttressed only by the vine, which had come to a diameter of seven and a half inches. By 1953, too, all the chimneys had disappeared, the main sills and first-floor boarding had rotted away, and several of the main walls had collapsed. Gone, as well, was the main stairway with its S-shaped carved step ends, so that there was no access to the rickety second floor. Although the ceiling of the Great Room was ready to collapse upon them, the cows loved the shade there on hot summer days. Before taking measurements and notes of this abode, the writer should have substantially increased his life insurance.

The *Frank Smith Place* was originally a part of *Long Neck* or *William's Fortune* and, according to its architecture, was probably erected in the middle of the eighteenth century. It was named for one of the old families of St. Mary's County—Smith. It was a Transitional house of the Late Cell type, with the aisles and symmetrical gables of that kind of building. The front porch with its brick floor and plaster ceiling was a later addition, although probably still eighteenth-century. The square posts were of interest, having chamfered edges and lamb's tongues and supporting elliptical arches. There were no dormers on the roof: all light and ventilation on the second floor and the tiny attic came from gable windows. The four chimneys had stepped weatherings and were laid up in the Flemish bond. From the shape of the two smaller chimneys, it was conjectured that there had been two upstairs fireplaces, although direct evidence was lacking. The roof had wooden shingles, and the weatherboarding comprised beaded clapboards, exposed six inches to the weather.

The stairway to the second floor, which was partially preserved elsewhere, avoided the use of winders. It had a square newel post beaded on all four corners, with a single capping; plain balusters, rectangular in section; and a rich nose molding and S-shaped spandrels or step ends. The little winding staircase to the attic took up more than half the width of the narrow passageway on the second floor, and had a miniature closet under it.

One of the most interesting features was the design of the opening between the Great Room and the stair passageway. In most early homes there would have been a door, or even an arch. Here, there is merely an opening four feet and seven inches wide, with a square head. There was no sign of a door. Even in that early style of house which modernists think of as being very antiquated, "space planning," where space "flows" from one room or area to another, was employed, as exemplified at the *Frank Smith Place*.

5. SPIRES OF *ST. ANDREW'S*

WHEN RICHARD BOULTON made the plans for *St. Andrew's Protestant Episcopal Church* in St. Mary's County in the year 1766, he designed that which we consider the most interesting Georgian church façade existing today in Maryland. The three spires which were planned and the twin towers separated by an enclosed porch form a scheme which, in Western ecclesiastical architecture, harks back to the early Chartres and to many cathedrals of the early Middle Ages.

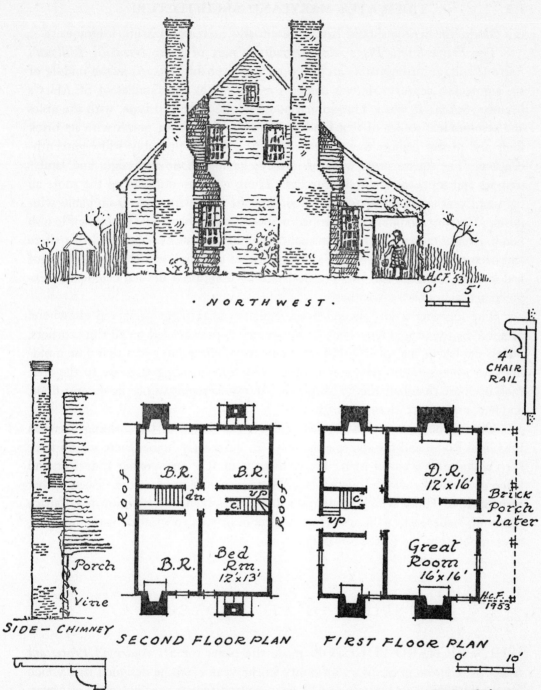

· N O R T H W E S T ·

H.C.F. 53

0'   5'

4"
CHAIR
RAIL

Roof

B.R.   B.R.

dn   up

c.

B.R.   Bed
Rm.
12'x13'

Roof

Porch

Vine

SIDE - CHIMNEY

SECOND FLOOR PLAN

D.R.
12'x16'

Brick
Porch
Later

up   c.

Great
Room
16'x16'

H.C.F.
1953

FIRST FLOOR PLAN

0'   10'

4" INTERIOR TRIM

meas. & drawn
H.C. Forman '54

Author's reconstruction of the FRANK SMITH HOUSE, St. Mary's County. In 1953
a great vine, 7½ inches in diameter, held up this dwelling, through which cows roamed
at will.

This church of *St. Andrew's* is hidden away in the St. Mary's woods, upon a side road, almost exactly as it was when built nearly two hundred years ago. Time has dealt mildly with this monument, and its interesting lines are still for anyone to see.

Richard Boulton's first scheme, dated April 17, 1766, to show the vestrymen of the church, was a building seventy feet long, exclusive of the chancel, and forty feet wide. But nine days later, on April 26, the vestry cut the length of *St. Andrew's* to fifty-five feet, "in the clear, exclusive of the chancel." That width remained unchanged (p. 115).

The building specification is of interest, and we shall transpose it largely into modern English for clarity, with our own explanations. The church was to be painted inside and out—but this requirement did not mean that the brickwork was to be painted. The pews were to be wainscoted—that is, paneled,—to be painted, and to have doors. The interior pillars were to be fluted and capped—that is, to have capitals. There were to be a handsome pulpit and reading desk. The aisles were to be laid with flagstones, and a handsome altarpiece of the Ionic order was to be erected. Two galleries were planned, and they were to be wainscoted. The portico or porch, on the west front, was to have two pyramids or steeples. The roof was to be planked, that is, sheathed, and was to be covered with cypress shingles. The exterior quoins were to be built up with stock bricks—which means that at the corners of the church ordinary English statute bricks were to be built to project out like cornerstones. In fact, all the exterior masonry was to be done with stock bricks.

The specification next turns its attention again to the interior. There were to be one arched ceiling—in other words, a barrel vault over the nave or central aisle—and two flat ceilings over the side aisles. Crown glass with "chemical" putty was to be employed for the windows. What the word "chemical" means is today anybody's guess.

The brick foundation was to be three and a half bricks thick; the wall between ground and water table three bricks thick; and from there to the eaves two and a half bricks thick. The height of the wall between the floor and the flat ceiling was to be fourteen feet.

The specification, meandering about in the language of those days, next returns to the subject of paint, stating that the exterior and interior, including the pews, were to be painted three times with white lead. The doors were to be folding—probably meaning doors of double leaves—and there were to be pulley weights for the double-hung window sash. The portico was to be laid up with brick set edgeways—evidently a reference to the manner of laying the floor. The church was to be finished by "Richard Boulton's Plann (the middle spire excepted)."

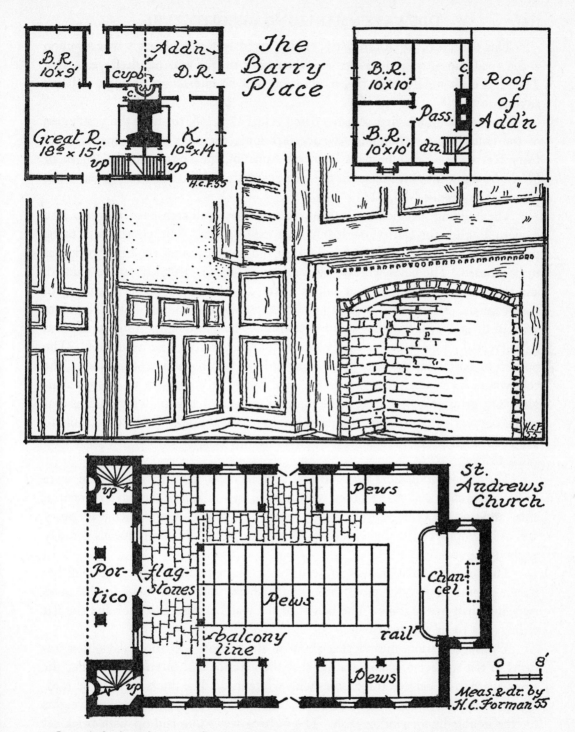

The Barry Place

B.R. 10'x9'   Add'n   D.R.
cupb.   c.

Great R. 18'6"x15'   K. 10'6"x14'
up   up
H.C.F. 55

B.R. 10'x10'   c.   Roof of Add'n
Pass.
B.R. 10'x10'   dn.

H.C.F. 55

St. Andrews Church
up
Por-tico   flag-stones   Pews   Chan-cel
Pews
balcony line   rail
Pews
up
0   8'
Meas. & dr. by H.C. Forman 55

One of the least-known early dwellings in Prince George's County is THE BARRY PLACE, with its fine woodwork in the Great Room. Below, a measured floor plan of ST. ANDREW'S EPISCOPAL CHURCH, St. Mary's County, built in 1766-67.

This is the most interesting item of the whole specification—a middle spire or *flêche*, which does not exist today, if it ever existed. Was it planned for surmounting the west gable, between the tower spires, or for crowning the high ridge at the east end of the church, where it could look down on the chancel roof? At any rate, the present tower spires are short and stubby. Since they seem to be out of proportion to the church, it is safe to surmise that they are replacements of the original ones. It is impossible to crawl up inside the tower spires to examine their structural timbers.

To continue with the old church records, we find that on May 3, 1766, Samuel Abell, Junior, contracted to build the church for 160,000 pounds of tobacco and 100 pounds sterling, and he entered into a bond for completion of the edifice. On June 18, 1768—over two years later—the vestry ordered Hugh Hopewell, "Esquire," to procure three barrels of turpentine, in order to tar the roof. The following year the pews were sold to the highest bidders, and Colonel George Plater received number one. One Richard Pooley agreed to make benches for the church—probably to be used in the balconies—and to find plank for them.

On March 29, 1770, the gentlemen of the vestry agreed to pay Hugh Hopewell ten pounds sterling "on account of Richard Boulton's overlooking the work done to the church"—that is, supervising the construction. But the records do not refer to him as architect, although he performed the duties of such.

And thus *St. Andrew's Church* was built. As we stand before its west front, we may see that the two square brick towers with stubby spires, the inset portico with twin square Doric piers, having entasis—that refined Greek bulging of a support—and the brick wall above the portico with Palladian window and triangular pediment form a screen to hide the whole gable end of the church proper. As we look more closely, we can see, too, that the Palladian window frame, pediment woodwork, and tower cornices are modern and crude replacements of the originals. Besides, the whole brick curtain wall above the portico is supported on a wooden beam across from tower to tower, and why it has not fallen in these nearly two hundred years is a puzzle. An interesting feature is the projecting of the Palladian window and its gable some four and a half inches from the wall—exactly like the central motif in many a late Georgian mansion.

On the west façade the towers have superimposed niches—that is, one niche is over another; and on the sides of the towers are superimposed shallow recessed arches—blind arches. Perhaps this scheme sounds complicated, but the photographs should explain (pp. 139, 141). At the corners of the towers the quoins rise only as high as the string course or fascia band marking the level of the second storey. The quoins also decorate the east gable but not the chancel.

The west front door and the two side doors have double leaves, and are arched with brick tympanums, the name for filling under the arches. The keystones and imposts, or spring blocks, are of raised brick. On the other hand, the windows do not have round arches, but segmental ones; and there are brick keystones.

All the walls of the church are laid up in Flemish bond of the best quality. When we come to examine in person the interior of the building, we find that little has been changed since 1767—perhaps the lack of improvements is its chief charm. The floor is beautifully paved with flagstones, the square columns are fluted with Ionic capitals, and the gallery is in two tiers—exactly as noted in the specifications. Reached by a stepladder a little more than three feet high, the upper deck, well lit by the Palladian window, was probably occupied during services by slaves. Access to this upper level was also gained by an outside door in one of the towers, a winding staircase, and a five-and-a-half-foot-high doorway cut into the plastered barrel vault of the nave.

The altarpiece, above the altar, was specified to be handsome and of the Ionic order—and it is all of that. "Handsome," if you will, in an eighteenth-century sort of way, it was carved in wood by John Freich Leinner. Fluted Ionic pilasters, of which the lower portions are reeded, support a broken pediment of semicircular design carrying small modillions and a pineapple (p. 140). Within this enframement are four tablets painted on vertical boards containing the following subjects, reading from left to right: the Lord's Prayer, Exodus, the Ten Commandments, and the Apostles' Creed. These tablets have a curvilinear hood painted a golden brown and a kind of scrollwork in gold on each side of the hood.

The proscenium arch or chancel opening has imposts carrying small modillions, which run the depth of the chancel. Also this arch has a large keystone at the summit. The chancel rail with turned balusters stands on a raised step above the flagstone floor, and there is a further step into the chancel itself. The doors of the pews have each a small and a large panel and originally were hung on butterfly hinges.

In the 1770s the churchyard was enclosed by a very substantial fence. On May 2, 1771, Samuel Bellwood, who had given the lot on which the church stood, agreed to make for the vestry a railing and four gates in the yard of "*St. Andrew's Parish Church.*" The rails were to be white or box oak, and the posts of red cedar or locust—seven feet long and six-by-fours "at the least,"—were to have tarred tenons and pins. The four gates were to be each four feet wide, and their posts ten feet long with diamond heads. The pales for the gates were to be seven inches thick and three inches broad. When put together, the pales were to be let into the bars by means of dovetails. Each gate was to be arched over, to have iron latches, and to swing on iron hooks and eyes.

Because of their strength these gates at *St. Andrew's* must have lasted for many years. Up to the late 1800s the church was still in use, but after that time the membership dropped rapidly. *St. Andrew's* was closed, and services were held at *St. Peter's Chapel* in Leonardtown.

During the Maryland Tercentenary Celebration in 1934, some of the structure was repaired, and in 1942 the church was rededicated. It is to be hoped that the fane has entered a long renaissance. It also is not too much to expect that where necessary the exterior woodwork will someday be replaced correctly and with refinement.

6. HOUSE WITH THE PIECE OF FALSE FRONT

A COTTAGE IN Calvert County built in the Transitional Style and dating perhaps from the 1740s or '50s stands at the present writing in the last stages of dilapidation (p. 146). The Great Room of the earlier brick portion holds pigs, and the cell addition leans over dangerously. The doors, sash, and hardware have disappeared—not an unusual condition in Maryland or elsewhere in the United States. Our drawing shows the small chimney reconstructed and the two windows in the cell conjecturally placed (p. 119).

The cell addition or wing seems to have been a separate house of its own, because its studded wall has been placed up against the brick wall of the original portion. The winding staircase was moved from next the chimney in the Great Room to the cell, where it cuts across a window adjacent to the fireplace in the Great Room. A study of the floor plan will clear up this point.

Before its destruction the smaller fireplace was three feet wide—a size not capacious enough for the usual kitchen fireplace. Therefore it seems reasonable to believe that the original kitchen shanty stood next or opposite to the outside doorway on the east.

A curious feature is the roof of the addition, which makes up a kind of gambrel on the south side—literally what the French call a "bent leg." Thus the later ridge was higher than the ridge of the brick house. On the north side the roof was made long and low-pitched in order to allow for head room upstairs. But the most interesting portion of the roof is on the west or main façade, where a piece of false front or screening abuts the great chimney stack, concealing the gambrel effect visible on the east and south. This screening, while not large, is as medieval in its nature as that on the west front of Lincoln or any other Early English minister.

· E A S T ·   · S O U T H ·

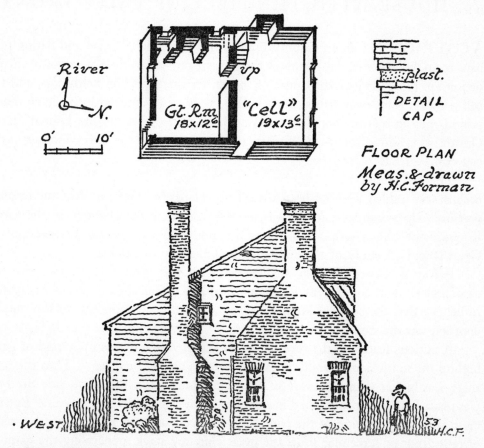

River

N.

0'   10'

Gt. Rm.
18x12⁶   "Cell"
19x13⁶

up

plast.

DETAIL
CAP

FLOOR PLAN
Meas. & drawn
by H.C. Forman

· W E S T ·   53   H.C.F.

In Calvert County, the HOUSE WITH THE PIECE OF FALSE FRONT *shows how eccentric the early style could be. Note the section of screening next to the large chimney on the east side.*

On the second floor at the head of the staircase runs a passageway four and a half feet wide the length of the brick portion of the dwelling, making the Hall Chamber, over the Great Room, long and narrow. This passage also opens on two bedrooms in the addition which are reached by descending two steps in each chamber.

There are those who may criticize the proportions of the cell addition, particularly as viewed from the east side. But its colonial crudity—perhaps its "Carpenter Colonial" naïveté—is superior to innumerable "modern" homes, the bad proportions of which are frequently seen nearly everywhere today.

The reader may successfully duplicate this house, if he wishes, as he would have an example of the genuine early style. Its picturesqueness portrays well that spirit of the Middle Ages which permeates early American architecture. But perhaps in this day and age there is no need for copying.

7. THE *PRIVATE JAIL* AND THREE QUAINT CHARLES COUNTY CHIMNEYS

EARLY MARYLAND had a number of jails, almost every one of which has disappeared. Gone without a trace is the log prison of 1663 in the early capital of Maryland, St. Mary's City. In the same settlement, the 1676 brick jail has now gone underground, as has most of that buried city. The windows, two downstairs and one in the loft, were built into the walls so strongly that no prisoner could possibly dislodge them, and there were 1¼-inch wrought-iron bars set vertically and horizontally. There was a partition across the middle of the downstairs space and an outside door for each section. Behind the jail was a ducking stool, which hung out over water. Such was the strongest prison in the Free State one hundred years before the American Revolution.

Sometimes the counties did not have sufficient funds at the moment to build an adequate number of jails; other times the prisons in existence became unsafe. Consequently a sheriff might erect a private jail from his own pocketbook. There is such a building, the *Private Jail*, now leaning heavily before it takes the final plunge, situated upon the Broderick tract, part of *St. John's Manor*, St. Mary's County.

In length this prison, a wooden, weatherboarded affair, almost matches that of the 1676 brick jail at St. Mary's City—twenty-four feet—but the width is only twelve feet, or three feet less. There once probably stood a partition in the middle; but that supposition is open to question, so the feature has been omitted from the floor plan (p. 122).

On the front there are two doors, of different sizes and ages, and two small shuttered windows, without glass—true "wind-holes," also of different ages and dimensions. There may have been a "wind-hole" in the center of the rear side, where the present modern window is situated.

Before Father Time took care of most of them, the original clapboards, ship-lap boards, were up to fifteen inches wide. The whole framework of the jail is hard oak, pegged and tenoned together. The studs and joists are set close enough so that no person could worm his or her way through them. There appears to be no brick foundation: the old wood sills, now crumbled, rest directly upon the ground.

But the chief attraction of this jail is finding out how His Lordship, the High Sheriff, locked in his prisoners. The left-hand doorway, the older of the two door-ways, has a batten door exactly three inches thick (details, p. 122). The outer, one-inch boards run vertically; the inner, two-inch boards are horizontal. The door has two great strap hinges hung on pintles which go clear through the frame of the door and have iron wedges to keep people from pulling them out. A wrought-iron lock, some fourteen inches long, is concealed in the boards of the door; and a great key, now lost, turned the lock. Now, of course, a door—even a heavy door, like this one—could be lifted off its pintles by an outsider, and the occupants of the prison could then escape. Therefore the door was additionally locked by a large iron bar, at one end bolted into the frame of the doorway and at the other end fastened by a big hasp and a giant padlock.

Nevertheless, the Sheriff did not consider the above arrangements adequate, for at some later date than the time of erection of the building he constructed an inner doorway, the frame of which was let into the frame of the outside door-way. This inside door, now gone, was 1¾ inches thick and had a rim lock upon its outer surface.

If anyone thinks it was easy to break out by the left-hand door, let him con-sider the left-hand window, the larger and older of the two windows on the front. For one thing, it was impossible to get yourself through the nine-inch-wide space, even if the four heavy iron bars in the window were cut in two. Besides, the small shutter, like the door, is three inches thick. Of three thicknesses of battens, bolted and riveted to two strap hinges, the shutter, like the door, could be barred on the exterior and locked with a hefty padlock.

How the poor devils kept warm in winter is anyone's guess. There is not the slightest evidence of a fireplace. In that age the best thing to do in the cold months was to stay good.

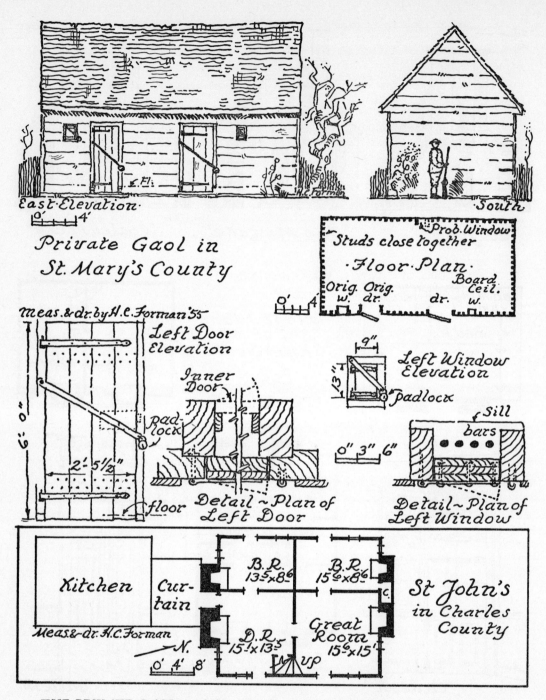

East Elevation · 0' 4'

South

Private Gaol in St. Mary's County

Prob. Window

Studs close together

· Floor Plan ·

Orig. Orig.   Board Ceil.
w. dr.   dr.   w.

0' 4'

meas. & dr. by H.C. Forman '55

Left Door Elevation

Inner Door

padlock

6' 0"

2'-5½"

floor

Detail ~ Plan of Left Door

9"

13"

Left Window Elevation

padlock

0" 3" 6"

Sill

bars

Detail ~ Plan of Left Window

Kitchen

Cur-tain

B.R. 13⁵ x 8⁶

B.R. 15⁶ x 8⁶

St John's in Charles County

Meas.& dr. H.C. Forman

N.

0' 4' 8'

D.R. 15¹ x 13⁵

Great Room 15⁹ x 15¹

UP

THE PRIVATE GAOL, *probably 200 years old, on Broderick, St. Mary's County. Notice how the High Sheriff of the county made security doubly secure by iron bars placed across openings and fastened by padlocks. Below, partially reconstructed first-floor plan of ST. JOHN'S, Charles County, noted for an arch through chimneys.*

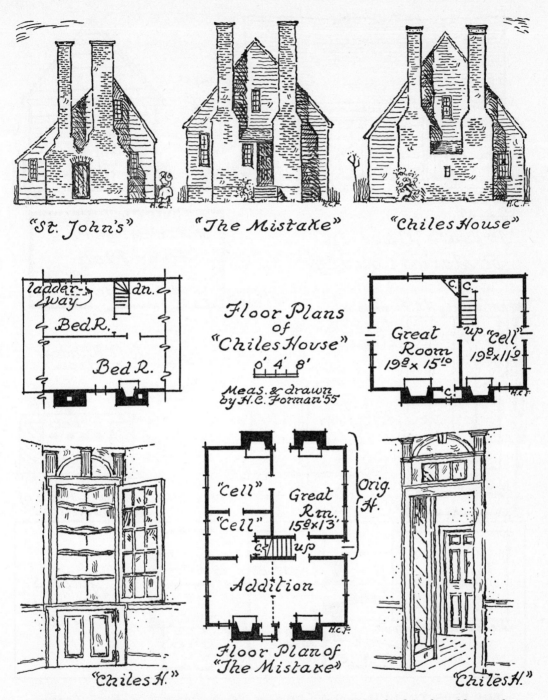

"St. John's" "The Mistake" "Chiles House"

Floor Plans
of
"Chiles House"
0' 4' 8'

Meas. & drawn
by H.C. Forman '55

ladder-way   dn.
Bed R.
Bed R.

C. C.
Great
Room
19⁸ x 15¹⁰   "up "Cell"
19⁸ x 11⁹

"Cell"
"Cell"   Great
Rm.
15⁸ x 13'   Orig.
H.

C.   up

Addition

Floor Plan of
"The Mistake"

"Chiles H."   "Chiles H."

One of the charms of domestic architecture in Southern Maryland is the widespread use of the outside chimney as the key factor in design. These three Charles County cottages of Transitional Style are excellent examples of such design. At bottom are sketches of cupboard and inside doorway in the REVEREND CHILES HOUSE.

We present here three small Charles County dwellings marked by picturesque chimneys. They are all in various states of repair. In the Great Room of at least one house snakes crawl at leisure and undisturbed.

One of the charms of domestic architecture in Southern Maryland is the widespread use of the exterior chimney as the key factor in design. One of these dwellings is *St. John's* (p. 143), which possibly belonged to John Stone, son of Governor William Stone, mentioned elsewhere in this volume. However, there were two other *St. John's* in the same county. At any rate, one Thomas Dyson, Senior, in 1710 is supposed to have owned the land on which the subject of this sketch was erected. There is a possibility that the footstone with the initials, AWD, lying in a nearby briar patch, belongs to one of the Dysons.

The feature of *St. John's*, a Transitional house of Early Cell type and catslide roof, is the arched doorway through the southwest double chimney, somewhat in the manner of *Society Hill*, in the same county. This arched door could be seen in its entirety at *St. John's* only after the kitchen-curtain wing had disappeared many years ago. Outlines of this wing may still be discerned in the grass.

The front doors of the abode are made of random-width, beaded battens. On the outside of each door the framework of styles and rails forms two vertical panels. The inside of the doors are smooth horizontal boards. The mantels are of plain, eighteenth-century type, with no ornament. The winding staircase from the garret rooms winds down into the Great Room, not next to the fireplace but uniquely in the center of the front façade (p. 122). The diagonal bottom step juts into this Great Room.

A second Charles County dwelling, with great chimneys, is known by the amusing name of *The Mistake* (p. 123). It was built in the eighteenth century by a member of the Reeves family on a tract called *Part of the Mistake*, and at that time it comprised only a section of the present residence. In October, 1825, one Thomas C. Reeves died there at the age of seventy.

The house has been much changed, what with moving a partition here and adding something there. The completed floor plan (p. 123) shows a Hangover Transitional home of Late Cell type, with a wood-boxed staircase and some open beams in the ceilings of the original part. The twin chimneys separated by a square-headed doorway and small closet with window, shown in the drawing, are the feature of the place, and form part of the addition to the original section.

The third chimneyed domicile (p. 143) is tucked away so far back in the Charles County forests that it is very difficult to find. This is the *Reverend Chiles House* (1770-80), once belonging to a man of that name who is reputed to have died in 1874. He must have liked the quiet life, because this home stands in a really lonesome spot. A good example of Hangover Transitional of Late Cell type, the cottage originally possessed downstairs only the Great Room with a cell room behind it. Some time in the early nineteenth century a porch was added to the front, and another porch and little room—an outshut—were joined to the house at the rear. The two chimneys rise at one gable and have a pent with small window between them. The outside walls are brick nogged, and the roof still carries the fish-scale shingles with which it was originally covered. Later shingling concealed these fish-scales.

The garret is reached by a boxed staircase rising from the cell room. The bottom step has an arched door opening into this room. A three-pane transom over the inner doorway to the Great Room helps to light the lower steps of this staircase.

Upstairs are two bedchambers and a small stair passage. But it is in the Great Room woodwork that much of the charm of the house lies, for there we have a diagonal cupboard with a molded arch, flanked by stubby, fluted pilasters (p. 123). Somewhat the same arched motif decorates the inner door of the Great Room and marks this humble cottage as no ordinary one.

8. *POYNTON MANOR*, HOME OF THE THIRD GOVERNOR OF MARYLAND

SHOWN HERE ARE two old photographs (p. 144), probably the only existing record of *Poynton Manor*, the original section of which was erected about 1654 by William Stone, Maryland's third Governor. For transporting into the Province himself, his wife, four children, and four servants, and for laudable services, William Stone, a Protestant vestryman who served as one of six Commissioners for the Eastern Shore of Virginia, received from Lord Baltimore 5000 acres on the Potomac River, in Nanjemoy Hundred, Charles County, Maryland. This great tract of about eight square miles, known as *Poynton Manor*, but sometimes called *Nanjemoy Manor*, was laid out on July 12, 1654, and on September 1, 1658, was granted him.

Poynton Manor has a long history, but perhaps it is fitting to consider first the house itself. It stood on that part of the manorial grant called Molly Stone's field and is reported to have burned down somewhere around the year 1740. Later it was rebuilt on the same site.

Now, upon close examination of the charming but obscure photographs of this dwelling, we find that the brick chimney pent and the right-hand chimney were later additions. The chimney on the left probably belonged to William Stone's house. As is often the case in homes of this style, like the *Leigh House*, St. Mary's City, Stone's lodging was afterward doubled in size. The porch and the wing on the right side with the pent roof—a perfect outshut—are probably excrescences of the nineteenth century.

It is not difficult to guess the floor plan. A passageway extended the whole depth of one gable end, with a Great Room and a dining room at the chimney end. Later the dining room was extended outward and the outshut added. Upstairs there were probably three tiny knock-heads and a slit passageway—reminiscent of those in *St. Barbara's*, Mistress Troughton's domicile in St. Mary's City.

But the original Stone house comprised only the Great Room and the front or forepart of the passageway, which may have been used as a parlor.

In Molly Stone's field there stood in recent times several tombstones, some of which had the name of Brauner.

The passing of *Poynton Manor* from father to son by the name of Stone for at least one hundred and fifty years may be traced in the old records. Governor William Stone, the immigrant, was an eminent landholder in St. Mary's City, the first capital. He owned the earliest-known property in that city—East St. Mary's, or the Governor's Field. In 1647 he was accused of unlawfully taking ownership of the Calvert or Governor's house in this Field.[1] In spite of that charge, the following year he became Governor and lived in the Calvert house a number of years. In truth, after *Poynton Manor* was built, he possessed two homes—no doubt with all the inconveniences thereto attached—and for several years after his death the seat in the Governor's Field in St. Mary's City was spoken of as Captain Stone's house at St. Mary's.

In 1660 he died, leaving the aforementioned town house and land in the Maryland capital to his wife, Verlinda Cotton. She was to remain at the dwelling plantation at *Poynton Manor* during her widowhood. According to the terms of his will, 600 acres of this manor went to his daughter Elizabeth, wife of William Calvert, son of the first Governor, Leonard Calvert. Five hundred acres went to each of his sons, Richard, John, and Mathew; and what remained of the manor was bequeathed to his oldest son, and residuary legatee, Thomas Stone.

The dwelling plantation next came into the possession of John Stone, son of Governor William; and then of Thomas and Walter Stone, son of John, who were to have equal shares in the dwelling and land, a 500-acre portion of *Poynton Manor*. After his mother's death, Walter Stone was to own that part whereon the habitation stood.

[1] *Jamestown and St. Mary's*, pp. 214, 215.

In 1725 the manor was divided into sections owned by Thomas Stone, William Stone, Mat Stone, Gerrad Fowke, Jesse Doyne, and William Doyne. David Stone, great-grandson of Governor William, is supposed to have been living at *Poynton Manor* at the time in which the dwelling was destroyed and to have had it rebuilt. His first wife was Mary Hanson, sister of the Honorable John Hanson, president of the Federal Congress in 1781, who lived at *Mulberry Grove* near Port Tobacco. His second spouse was Elizabeth Jenifer, sister of the Honorable Daniel of St. Thomas Jenifer (1723-90). Thomas Stone, the "Signer" of "Havre de Venture," Charles County, was a son by his second wife.

In short, from Governor William Stone's little two-room-and-loft cottage came one of the most distinguished families of the United States. Our nation rose from just such small beginnings as *Poynton Manor*.

9. SPRIGG'S *NORTHAMPTON* AND L'ENFANT'S GARDEN

ONE OF THE important estates of Prince George's County is *Northampton*, a tract of 1000 acres surveyed on May 26, 1673, for Thomas Sprigg I, born in Northamptonshire, England, and who later became High Sheriff, Justice, and Commissioner of Calvert County, Maryland. He was married twice, first to Katherine Roper, a sister-in-law of Governor William Stone of Maryland, then to Eleanor Nuthall, a granddaughter of John Nuthall, who owned the Manor of Cornwaleys Crosse and St. Elizabeth's Manor near St. Mary's City.

When Sprigg died in 1704 he bequeathed to his son, Thomas II, "my dwelling home and all houses and land of 'Northampton' and 'Rolling' that I have not disposed of, and one part of five hundred acres of land I patented for me The Manor of Collington." In 1707, fifty acres of *Northampton* were possessed by Thomas Brooke, and 850 by Thomas Sprigg II.

It is evident that the timber-framed gambrel-roofed house which stood on the *Northampton* tract had been erected by Thomas Sprigg I before his death in 1704. The dwelling may very well have been seventeenth-century in date. It was described as being 125 feet in length. In the forepart were a withdrawing room, a library, and a dining room, all having high chimney pieces and wide, open fireplaces. At the rear were bedrooms which were later lit by tall Victorian-Gothic windows. In 1788—so it has been stated—a gambrel-roofed addition with tiny windows and broad clapboards was placed nestling against a main gable.

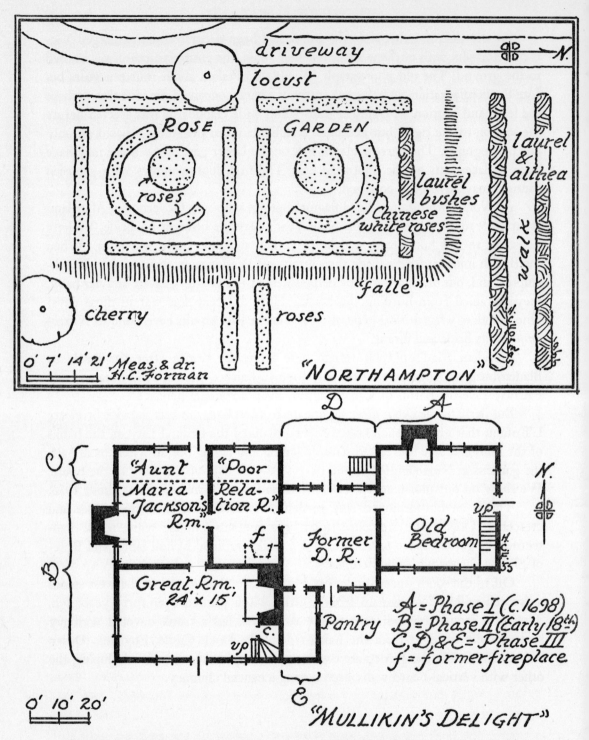

Author's measured plot plan of the garden at NORTHAMPTON, reputed to have been designed in 1788 by Pierre L'Enfant. Below, first floor plan of MULLIKIN'S DELIGHT, built in three stages.

At any rate, in 1909, after the abode had been decorated with enlarged Victorian dormers with curlicue rakes on their roofs, the entire structure was burned to the ground. The old photograph (p. 148) was taken about fourteen years before the conflagration. After some study, we have conceived the idea that perhaps the left-hand portion with tiny windows and wide clapboards was erected before the section to the right, but certainty is difficult when the study is based on only one photograph. The narrow clapboards on the larger part of the home may have been replacements of the Victorian era. The first-floor windows with jalousied shutters may have been enlarged.

At *Northampton* once lived Samuel Sprigg, who was Governor of Maryland from 1819 to 1822. In 1811, on New Year's Day, he brought his bride, Violette Lansdale, to this homestead; and in 1812 their daughter Sally was born. When the British military forces made their attack on Washington, they came to Northampton and, out of regard for the helplessness of the young Violette and her baby, they refrained from burning the house. How different was war in those days! One wonders what a Nazi general or a Chinese Red would have done to *Northampton*, its bride and infant.

President Madison took refuge here from the British after the Battle of Bladensburg on August 14, 1814. Dr. John C. Fairfax, who in 1869 became Lord Fairfax, Twelfth Baron of Cameron, also made his home here.

But perhaps the event most significant to *Northampton* was the visit of Pierre L'Enfant, that great French engineer who planned the Federal City on the banks of the Potomac. He is credited with designing and laying out, in whole or in part, the gardens at Northampton in the year 1788—the date of the wing of the house. We show on our plot plan (p. 128) what remained of these gardens about 1936.

This is an old-fashioned rose garden in two squares, enclosing circles and crescents. One of the crescent-shaped beds contains Chinese white roses. Protecting the garden space on the north is a walkway lined by tall laurel and Rose-of-Sharon shrubs with thick trunks.

Off to the south once stood a little brick schoolhouse, and to the west stands a "switch willow," grown up from a little switch planted over forty years ago. The great locust tree, adjacent to the rose beds, has a trunk covered with ivy sentimentally brought from the Fairfax domicile, Leeds Castle, England. Down the hill and below the garden are two large slave quarters, one a brick duplex, the other with vertical-board walls, each having a central chimney.

10. THE DELECTABLE *MULLIKIN'S DELIGHT*

HIDDEN AWAY upon a hillock in Prince George's County stands *Mullikin's Delight*, a dwelling which has grown up in three successive stages. We find that on October 11, 1683, the *Mullikin's Delight* land, comprising 300 acres, was surveyed for John Keen, and that it was resurveyed fifteen years later, on October 14, 1698, for James Mullikin, second of that name in Maryland. The original patent declared that this land was to be taken out of that part of the Proprietary's Manor of Calverton on the western branch of the Patuxent River,

> next adjoining the land of John Darnall, with the yearly rent at the two most usual feasts of the year, viz., the Annunciation of the Blessed Virgin Mary and St. Michael, the Archangel, by even and equal portions the rent of twelve shillings sterling in silver or gold.

In repairing and modernizing this habitation, the present owners found that the whole structure had been built curiously irregularly. For example, the chimneys were set at all kinds of angles. The two small snapshots (p. 149) which they took in the 1930s show somewhat the problems which they faced in their project. One snapshot shows what is believed to be the earliest portion, dating from about 1698, and showing brick nogging between the studding where the clapboards have been torn away, a construction which is to all intents and purposes half-timber work. This is the first *Mullikin's Delight* house, which has been labelled Phase I on the floor plan (p. 128) and of which we have drawn a sketch.[1] When all the additions were made, this earliest portion became known as the Old [Master] Bedroom, or the East Wing. We do not believe that it ever served as the original kitchen, because its fireplace was not large enough. Besides, the site of the original kitchen is believed to have been to the north of this lodging. Unfortunately, the batten doors, fireplace, staircase and closet have been removed from this earliest portion, so that our drawing is really a reconstruction.

The second stage of development, Phase II on the floor plan, comprises the cottage erected in the early eighteenth century to the west of the first house. This became the main house and was built in the Transitional Style of Late Cell type. That is, there were little chambers at the back of the Great Room, and the gables were symmetrical.

The final, important Phase III, was first, the extending rearward six feet of the two back cells or aisles—as may be proven by the roof construction visible in the attic—and second, the building of a large curtain or passageway, which served

---

[1] See also *The Architecture of the Old South,* fig. 207.

the purpose of a dining room, connecting the first house with the main block. About this time, too, a wart or outshut, which used to function as a pantry, was stuck on the south side of the curtain, making the floor plan of the ensemble more irregular and quaint than ever.

The builders liked to place outside chimneys off center with the gable, as they did in the earliest portion and in one of the back cells known as Aunt Maria Jackson's Room. In the other cell, delightfully called the Poor Relation Room—harking back to that day when homes were few and relatives were many—the fireplace in a normal house would have been catercornered. But this one (now gone) was built at right angles to the fireplace in the Great Room—a unique example in Maryland.

The Great Room fireplace itself is arched and is five feet wide in span and three feet deep. At its right is a small fireplace closet, which has been altered, and a break-your-neck staircase, which leads to three sloping-ceiling bedrooms. The ceiling of the Great Room is beamed, with beaded boards across it.

From the roof came some ancient shingle souvenirs, which form the most unusual single item on the plantation. These cedar shingles are about four feet long, five inches wide, and they were laid upon the roof horizontally, as may be seen by the position of the nail holes. When in position on the roof, their upper edges were "knife edges."

On hot summer days the fine old trees form a shady and protective covering about the domicile. In the background lies the graveyard,[2] hidden by periwinkle and yews. There are no seventeenth-century tombstones remaining. The owners believe that in the seventeenth century the graves were marked by wood plaques or boards.

From James Mullikin II, the place descended to his son, James III, who married Charity Belt and died in 1740, leaving the plantation to their son, James Mullikin IV. Many of the Mullikins are connected with the Bowie family, probably through the marriage of Mary Mullikin, daughter of James Mullikin II, the builder, in December, 1709, to John Bowie, Sr. This wedding is thought to have taken place at *Mullikin's Delight.*

The Mullikins had an earlier domicile, *Marriotts,* in Anne Arundel County—a tiny wood contraption with gambrel roof, which has been burned. If it were in truth earlier, it could have been no more quaint than this delightful retreat on the Prince George's County hilltop.

[2] The oldest stone is dated 1816: "To the Memory of Mrs. Ann M. Mullikin Consort of William B. Mullikin who departed the life March 31st 1816." Other stones are: John Contee Mullikin, son of John B. and Mary M. Mullikin, b. Oct. 21, 1824, d. May 28, 1858; John B. Mullikin, d. June 19, 1862, aged 72 years; Mary B. Mullikin, d. July 13, 1864, aged 70 years; Benjamin Oden Mullikin, "who went to his rest" Nov. 3, 1854, aged 31; Edith Jackson, b. Jan. 24, 1858, d. July 14, 1858; Ida, infant of James & H. Mullikin.

11. THE THREE SISTERS—A MANGLING
AND AN AMPUTATION

IN 1683 LORD BALTIMORE granted to Thomas Hilleary I a 1050-acre tract called *Three Sisters*. On this land, probably soon after that year was erected the small, wooden, gambrel-roofed dwelling still standing today (p. 141). This Thomas Hilleary, it may be noted, married Eleanor Sprigg, daughter of Thomas Sprigg I, and half niece of Governor Thomas Stone.

When Thomas Hilleary died in 1697, he left by will to his wife Eleanor a part of *Three Sisters*, and to his son John Hilleary another part of the same property. His daughters were named as follows: Mary Berry, Elizabeth Lyle, Frances Wilson, Verlinda, and Tabitha.

Not until some time in the nineteenth century did the house pass from the Hilleary family, and then to their relatives, the Magruders, who until about 1915 lived at that pleasant seat in Prince George's County.

At the moment of the writer's visit in 1939, *The Three Sisters* fireside was suffering from a mangling and amputation which can now be good cause for regret. The huge free-standing chimney seen in the photograph was being demolished brick by brick; and the south part of the dwelling—an addition to the original structure—was in the process of having its walls removed in order to be changed into a porch. Since 1939 much of the domicile has been "restored"— that is, using the word in quotation marks—but some of the original sash, beaded siding, and molded box cornices remain. The foundation is both brick and stone, and there is a little lie-on-your-stomach window up under the ridge.

The plan of the abode is simple: on the first storey, two rooms and passageway and a stair that is steep and plain. All the old mantels have gone, some having been chopped up for firewood. Likewise the many outbuildings have all been lost.

The Three Sisters is similar in shape and in several other respects to *Mount Pleasant*, also in Prince George's County, a seat illustrated in *Early Manor and Plantation Houses of Maryland*. The grandson of Thomas Hilleary I, who had the same name, or his great-grandson, Tilghman Hilleary, is reputed to have built *Mount Pleasant*. It is told that Tilghman Hilleary's son, Washington Hilleary, fought a duel with another man over a lady at the old duelling grounds at Bladensburg, and that ever afterward Washington was lame.

About a quarter of a mile southwest of *The Three Sisters* is the site of another old Hilleary house, destroyed by fire; but there remain two flat slabs marking the graves of Hillearys who were born in the eighteenth century. Still a third Hil-leary berth, apparently built before the American Revolution, stands in this area of Prince George's County—but that is another story.

12. *THE BARRY PLACE* AND *DRYAD HILL*— ON THE ROAD TO RUIN

ONE OF THE little-known homes of Prince George's County is the *Barry House*, noted for its fine wainscoting and unusual floor plan. Especially pleasing is the woodwork in the Great Room (p. 137), where at the fireplace side the overmantel extends to the ceiling, and on the other three sides the paneling rises about halfway to the top of the wall. The mantel itself has a low arch resembling that in the sitting room at *Araby* in Charles County; besides, it has the effect of dentils made by punctation.

The original dwelling was of the Transitional Style of Late Cell type, as may be seen in the floor plans (p. 115). Back of the Great Room are two tiny cells separated by a narrow passageway. A winding staircase rises beside the Great Room fireplace to an upstairs passage and two little knock-head bedrooms. On this upper floor there is but one closet for the whole family.

Still in the early days, a perfect example of what we call an outshut was added to the south gable, forming a shed the whole twenty-seven-foot width of the building (p. 137). This outshut contains a kitchen, located back of the Great Room fireplace, and a dining room which takes up a portion of one of the original cells. Further, a circular china cupboard was built in the dining room next to the Great Room fireplace, and a short piece of stairs from the kitchen joined the staircase to the loft. On the west side is a later porch, with brick terrace, and a well.

The reader may wonder why the *Barry Place* has been allowed to deteriorate. Its deplorable condition does not compare with that of *Dryad Hill* in Anne Arundel County. This homestead, which is almost all porch, needs the restorer's careful hand at once; otherwise the place will go down ruin's road to oblivion.

Home of the Ditty family for many years, it stands forlorn and forsaken, hidden by overgrown fields and uncut woods. Dilapidated outbuildings make a ring around the house, and the very air is full of decay. The older section of *Dryad Hill* (p. 150), one and a half storeys high, is late eighteenth-century in date, while the larger portion is nineteenth. It is curious that this larger section, while two storeys and attic high, is only one room thick, the rest of the space being taken up by porches. At the first-floor level there are verandahs on both sides. Upstairs, the south porch has been converted into a bedchamber, with blinds or jalousies which open and shut; and the north porch is small and partly plastered.

Before the floors began to sag, *Dryad Hill* plantation was the scene of a happy romance between Jacob Wheeler Bird and one of the Ditty young maidens. He and she spent many a pleasant hour, it is told, wandering about the grove of trees and in the garden of this untouched bower in Anne Arundel County. And in time they married.

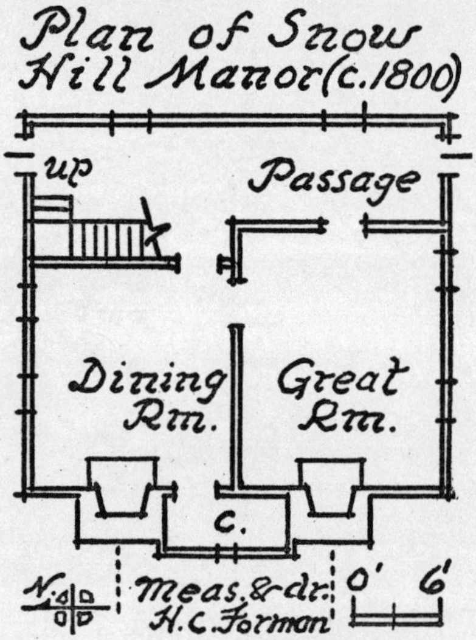

Plan of Snow Hill Manor (c. 1800)

up   *Passage*

Dining Rm.   *Great Rm.*

c.

N.   *meas. & dr.*   0'   6'
      H. C. Forman

The ROSE CROFT with its boxwood garden, St. Mary's City, first capital of Maryland, as the house appeared in the 1860s, after the gambrel roof was removed. Here lived His Majesty's Collector, Wolstenholme.

This view of the so-called *WOLSELEY MANOR*, St. Mary's County, is taken from the land or north side of the house. On the left of the doorway is a nineteenth-century addition. This was not Chancellor Philip Calvert's dwelling. Johnston.

In St. Mary's County, the FRANK SMITH HOUSE, mid-18th-century, is Transitional, of Late Cell type. The wing was later. Author, 1938. Below, is the BARRY HOUSE, Prince George's County. Note large "outshut."

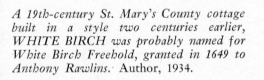

A 19th-century St. Mary's County cottage built in a style two centuries earlier, WHITE BIRCH was probably named for White Birch Freehold, granted in 1649 to Anthony Rawlins. Author, 1934.

In 1938 we photographed this brick-floored porch at the FRANK SMITH HOUSE. Note the elliptical arches, and the vine at the left which later engulfed the structure.

Built in 1767, ST. ANDREW'S EPISCOPAL CHURCH, near California, St. Mary's County, has the most interesting front of all the Georgian churches of Maryland. Each tower lower niche has a brick enframement. The stubby steeples are modern. Johnston.

The nave of *ST. ANDREW'S EPISCOPAL CHURCH*, St. Mary's County, is terminated by a triumphal arch under which the Commandments are framed by Ionic pilasters supporting a pulvinated frieze and circular pediment. Richard Boulton was the architect, and John Friech Leinner the carver of the altar-piece.

A recent view of the south side of ST. ANDREW'S CHURCH. Author, 1955. Below, *the THREE SISTERS dwelling, erected soon after 1683 on land granted by Lord Baltimore to Thomas Hilleary, I. Elizabeth Chandlee, author's little daughter, 1934.*

A bold, two-storey brick chimney-pent, lighted upstairs and down by small windows, embellishes LOCUST GROVE FARM (c.1790), Charles County. It is partly hidden by a later wing. Here lived John A. Burroughs, grandfather of the present owner.

In Charles County, the REVEREND CHILES HOUSE (c.1770-80) and the dwelling, ST. JOHN'S (below), are gaunt reminders of what is overtaking the early architecture of Southern Maryland. Author.

These two old faded photographs are probably the only existing record of *POYNTON MANOR* house, the first portion of which was built about 1654 by Maryland's third Governor, William Stone, on an eight-square-mile grant of land.

BRODERICK, a part of St. John's Manor, St. Mary's County, is a gambrel-roof house with brick chimney-pent of 18th-century vintage. It has also been known as the Patrick Russell or the Love farm. The addition on the right has been removed. Johnston.

The PIRATE HOUSE, St. Mary's County, of perhaps 1790-1810 period, has a penthouse between chimneys. At the time of the writer's visit, cows were eating inside all the outbuildings. Author, 1934. Below is author's recent photograph of THE HOUSE WITH THE PIECE OF FALSE FRONT, in Calvert County.

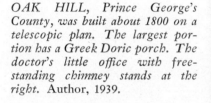

OAK HILL, Prince George's County, was built about 1800 on a telescopic plan. The largest portion has a Greek Doric porch. The doctor's little office with free-standing chimney stands at the right. Author, 1939.

SNOW HILL MANOR, near St. Mary's City, was built in the year 1803, with large brick chimney-pent closet and a Great Room mantel with a frieze of straps. Abel Snow's manor-house of Snow Hill existed in 1639. Author, 1934.

This old photograph shows NORTHAMPTON, Prince George's County, the first section of which is believed to have been erected about 1700. Home of Lord Fairfax. HABS, 1895. Below, *the brick slave quarters on a duplex design and with central chimney.* Author, 1939.

In Prince George's County, James Mullikin, II, about 1698 built the first portion of MULLIKIN'S DE-LIGHT, shown above. Wilfong. Below, are snapshots of the house before renovation. Kirtley.

The beamed Great Room in MULLIKIN'S DELIGHT, Prince George's County, is part of the second or 18th-century dwelling. Below—DRYAD HILL, Anne Arundel County,—a domicile which is almost all porch. Author, 1939.

4

UPPER BAY COUNTIES AND BALTIMORE

1. *FURLEY HALL* AND THE GREEN ROSES

IN the City of Baltimore at the eastern end of Brehms Lane, just beyond the bridge over Herring Run, lies the site of great *Furley Hall,* long the subject of fact and fiction. For over one hundred and twenty-eight years, before its partial destruction by fire in 1906, *Furley* was a Bowly homestead, then a Corse plantation. Here in 1953 took place the bulldozer "push" which leveled to the fields everything standing upon this property. The Romans could not have done a better job with Carthage. Yet *Furley Hall* was one of the most elegant country houses within the present limits of Baltimore, and one of the most interesting.

An old photograph published in *Early Manor and Plantation Houses of Maryland* (1934), and reproduced in larger fashion here (p. 184), shows the Best Parlor at *Furley* with its hand-carved Directoire mantel and French wallpaper of robin's-egg blue, bright flowers, birds, and hanging baskets. The mansion was built about 1775, and the wallpaper was brought from France in 1778.

In planning reconstruction drawings of *Furley,* we decided to use only old photographs (pp. 181, 182) and verbal descriptions given by members of the family which once lived there. But one day—it was March 22, 1952—we had a hunch that a visit to the site of vanished *Furley Hall* would be important. This feeling proved a fortunate idea, because enough material evidence remained on the plantation to supplement greatly the paper data.

Nevertheless, to find the site of the Hall was a difficult matter: the neighbor-

153

hood had so changed the periphery of the estate by means of crowded tenements and row houses that identification was hindered. Even streets had been changed around. Once having gained the Furley hill, we were pleasantly surprised to discover that a number of structures were still in existence, and we have entered them upon the plot plan (p. 159). These were the stone cellar of the main block of *Furley*, which had a Victorian domicile upon it; the brick kitchen wing, which was used as a stable for riding horses; the brick smoke house, which was in poor condition, also used as a stable; *Bowley's Quarters*, a small stone house covered with ivy and attached to a huge ugly wooden addition; the great stone barn, which was still in use; and, finally, the spring house, its ruins enshrouded with thick vegetation.

The dining-room wing of *Furley Hall* had completely vanished, cellar and all, so that the kitchen wing stood like an island to one side of the Victorian domicile. The impression had been given to the writer that *Furley Hall* had entirely disappeared; yet all these structures except the Victorian contraption have been incorporated into our drawings.

It has taken four years to collect and analyze the data on *Furley Hall*; but we feel that the hours of patient work piecing this puzzle together have been rewarded by reconstructions which rescue one of Baltimore's great mansions from oblivion.

The most surprising sight on a first visit to *Furley* in 1952 was how the place had changed from the good old days. Where once had flourished vast areas of neatly-cultivated gardens in the rich bottom lands of the Herring Run, there had grown up a huge, low-grade tenement. Our notes taken at the site well describe the place at this time: "A small colonial village turned into a mammoth patchwork slum of tin shanties, chicken-box hovels, and the like." It develops that one of the tenants of *Furley* in the not-too-distant past lived Scot free for a period of years and had made the old Quaker home place into a money-maker. He ran a riding academy and a chicken farm among other activities. He subleased rooms, outbuildings, and shanties which he himself had thrown together.

So much trash had been spread helter-skelter over the *Furley* grounds that looking for relics of the plantation was a decidedly unpleasant experience. The dark and musty cellar of the main block of the original mansion was choked with immense cobwebs through which we had to take our measurements. This basement is clean enough in our drawing (floor plan, p. 155), and the ordeal of getting around inside this long-unvisited cellar fortunately does not show.

In short, what *Furley* had become by 1952 was scarcely to be believed on sight. Although modern city blocks surrounded the farm, modern sanitation laws stopped at its borders.

· SOUTHEAST · ELEVATION ·

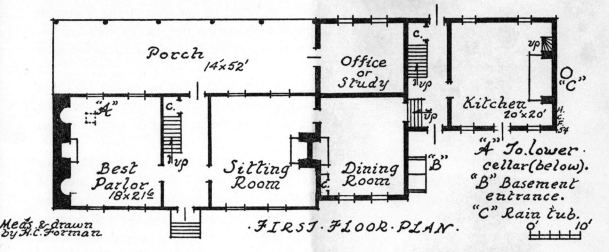

Porch 14'x52'

Office or Study

c.

up

up

"C"

Kitchen 20'x20'

H. C. F. '54

"A"

c.

up

Best Parlor 18'x21½

Sitting Room

Dining Room

c.

"B"

"A" To lower cellar (below).

"B" Basement entrance.

"C" Rain tub.

Meas & drawn by H.C.Forman

· FIRST · FLOOR · PLAN ·

0'   10'

Author's reconstruction of the mansion and barn, FURLEY HALL, Baltimore City. The refined Georgian style of the 1770s, with Ionic pilasters, fan transom, modillion cornices, and bull's eye windows.

The "Furley Hall" Stone Barn (restored), 75'-4" x 30' in size

H.C.F.

0'   8'

Then came May 14, 1953, a sad day in the history of *Furley Hall*. A development concern sent bulldozers to strip the garden behind what was left of the original mansion. We know: we were there. The garden itself was ploughed up, and many of the shanties went down like a pack of cards. The great trees fell with thundering crashes.

At this particular time, the tenant in the outbuilding called *Bowley's Quarters*, who was on the very verge of removal, refused this writer permission to enter his lodging to secure measurements. With demolition perhaps only hours away, his refusal was especially unkind. The reason given was that his furniture had not yet been removed. But even when his poor effects had gone, this tenant kept his doors locked, with a giant police dog inside. Finally, after he had vacated *Bowley's Quarters*, and after the neighborhood vandals had smashed every pane in the cottage and as much more of the fabric as they could lay their hands upon, this writer effected an entrance—not without some trepidation that the snarling hound might be upstairs. That was a timely entrance, because the bulldozers were even then making preparations to level the great stone barn and every other object standing above ground.

Thus in the great city of Baltimore, where the shade trees are slowly diminishing in number and where the water table is becoming lower, the giant Cedar of Lebanon, shown on our plot plan of *Furley Hall*, was crushed to make room for the slums of the future. May 14, 1953, was *Furley's* red-letter day.

This destruction of an important country seat in the middle of one of our great modern cities has been described in this way in order to leave for posterity not only a record of its existence, but also of what man has done to it.

The builder of *Furley Hall* mansion was Daniel Bowly II (1745-1807), who is believed to have constructed it to resemble the Bowly homestead in England. This Daniel Bowly was the son of Daniel Bowly I, who in 1745 settled in Baltimore and who in 1744 married Elizabeth Lux, daughter of Captain Darby Lux, of 43-44 Light Street. Captain Darby's house may be seen on the engraving of Baltimore of 1752 "drawn by John Moale, Esq., and corrected by Daniel Bowly, Esq."

The builder of *Furley* was himself a prominent merchant of Baltimore, an active patriot in the American Revolution, and a large landowner. Among other things, he was Town Commissioner from 1771 to 1778 and State Senator at three different times. With his uncle, William Lux, he formed the importing and shipowning firm of Lux and Bowly. His town house stood at the corner of Water and South Streets.

The wife of Daniel Bowly II, builder of *Furley*, was Anne Stewart, daughter of Captain Alexander Stewart and Sarah Lane Lux, his wife and first cousin. The marriage took place in 1775. Anne, it seems, was considered the most beautiful woman of the Baltimore area. A portrait of her was painted by Sir Joshua Reynolds from a miniature. Some of her attractions were auburn hair, blue eyes, and a "wonderfully" fair skin. Such was the first mistress of *Furley*.

Of the extensive lands which Daniel II owned at the time of his death, there were 2563 acres in Baltimore County, of which *Furley*, not yet enclosed by the city, had 793. On Middle River in Baltimore County he possessed the 450 acres of *Bowley's Quarters*—a fact which accounts for the building by that name on the home place.

Daniel II forms the subject of an oil painting by Charles Willson Peale which hangs in the Maryland Historical Society. The English landscape artist, Francis Guy, painted him and David Harris together in another oil. This same Francis Guy is reputed to have made a landscape of *Furley Hall*, but the whereabouts of the canvas is not known.

Eleven children were born to Daniel and Anne (Stewart) Bowly. One of them, Ann Lux Bowly, was born at *Furley* and in 1798 married Henry Thompson of *Clifton* on the Harford Road, Baltimore. It was at a ball in Baltimore that Thompson, from England, met Ann Lux. He was introduced to her by a Miss Hudson, who is reputed to have said: "Nanny! I am going to introduce to you a handsome young Englishman, but you must not fall in love with him. I want him myself." The result of this meeting was that young Thompson fell in love with Ann Lux—a love which was reciprocated. According to the custom, her father, the builder of *Furley Hall*, wrote to his father to ask consent to the marriage.

The name *Furley* is an old one in the Bowly family and was originally spelled De Fuylle. At the Battle of Poitiers in 1365 one Sir Richard de Beaulieu, a Bowly progenitor, was killed, along with a close friend, one Sir William De Fuylle. The name of the Bowly's English home near Bristol is supposed to have been *Furley*, and there were Bowlys living in it as late as 1805.

In 1814 *Furley* was the scene of war: soldiers from the British army forcibly occupied the premises. Then in 1847 the place was purchased by William Corse, Sr., a Friend who had been born in *Phillip's Purchase*, the Rigbie House, near Darlington, Harford County. His parents were John Corse, Jr., and Susannah Coale Corse; his grandparents John and Cassandra (Rigbie) Corse (Coursey), of *Hebron*, Kent County, on the Eastern Shore. Cassandra was the daughter of Colonel James Rigbie, High Sheriff of Baltimore County, and his wife, Elizabeth Harrison, of *Holly Hill*, Anne Arundel County.[1] Thus after 1847 another prominent family occupied *Furley Hall*.

The new owner, William Corse, Sr., was husband of Deborah Sinclair, whose

[1] Forman, H. C., *The Turner Family of Hebron and Betterton, Maryland* (1933).

father, Robert Sinclair, Sr., lived at *Clairmont*, situated across Herring Run from *Furley*. When Lafayette visited Baltimore in 1824, a reception was given him in the old Town Hall, and a silver cup as a prize was awarded to that person who offered the finest horticultural exhibit. Winner of the cup and two silver medals was this Robert Sinclair, who had them from the hand of the French general himself. It is probable that Lafayette visited the Sinclair nurseries at *Clairmont* and gave Robert Sinclair a present of two salt cellars on a silver tray.

William Corse, Sr., and Deborah Sinclair were married on April 13, 1831, at the Lombard Street Friends' Meetinghouse in Baltimore, and they had four boys and six girls: Mary, Caroline (born in New York), Robert (born in the Rigbie House), George Fox, Esther (or Hester), Susan, William, Annie (born at *Clairmont*), Frank, and Lucy. Another son, Henry Clay, died in infancy.

A chatty letter from Deborah Sinclair Corse to her sister Anne, who was Mrs. John Foulke, written at New York, July 2, 1831, soon after her marriage with William Corse, Sr., mentioned that she was very much pleased with that city.

> We have a house about the size of Brundige's in Sharp Street [Baltimore] with every convenience, folding doors, both rooms carpeted alike & everything plain and neat, something like yours when you first went to housekeeping. I have attended to thy advice about not making acquaintance too hastily as those were my sentiments exactly. We have had a great deal of company the short time we have been housekeeping. I find Uncle John's family very kind, & as we live some distance apart, I think we will get along very well. Rebecca Turner [who was Rebecca Sinclair Turner, her first cousin] and Mary Bartlett attended our Y[early] Meeting which was about a month since they were to see us several times. They were very anxious to see how I would look at the head of a table.... I wish thee was only here to accompany us to the sea shore next week. We expect to make a company to go with us. The place where we are going is a very fashionable resort, & I expect there will be a great many persons there as the weather is so warm. I am as happy at present as I could ever wish to be in this world. I think as thee used to tell me, that the married life was the most happy, but at that time I could not believe it. We had a very small wedding. Joseph Turner [Jr.] read the [marriage] certificate & it was written by a celebrated writing-master in New York. William [the groom] spoke quite audibly, but I was so much frightened & agi[tated] that I was not heard by one person. I had a very light dove coloured Gabinette dress, a spencer [overcoat] made of folds of gauze & satin, a long gauze scarf with satin embroidered ends, black shoes and white satin hat. I. L. Roberts & Cassandra Corse waited on us! Sisters L., H., & Betsy sat on the bench before us. We left Baltimore the next morning & sisters L. & Hetty went as far as the Canal with us. We remained in Phila. 3 days. It was in the

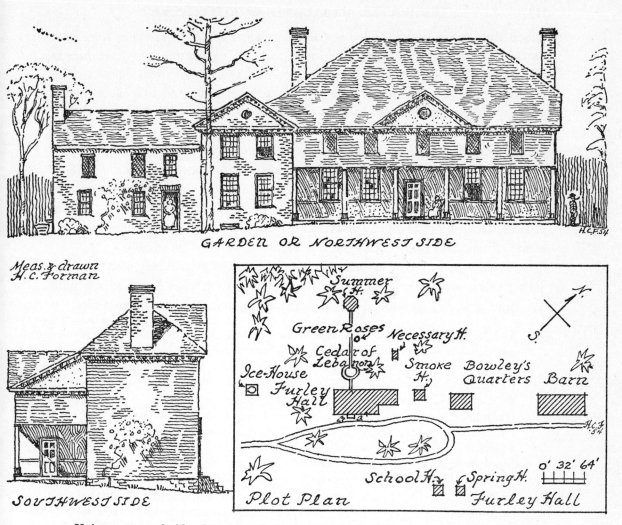

GARDEN OR NORTHWEST SIDE

Meas. & drawn
H. C. Forman

SOUTHWEST SIDE

Plot Plan
Furley Hall

Summer H.
Green Roses
Cedar of Lebanon
Ice-House
Furley Hall
Necessary H.
Smoke H.
Bowley's Quarters
Barn
School H.
Spring H.

0' 32' 64'

Unique rear and side elevations of FURLEY HALL, *Baltimore City, first a Bowly home and later belonging to the Corses. In the plot plan may be seen the noted bush of green roses.*

week of Y[early] Meeting & we saw a great many friends we knew, which made it rather more cheerful for me after leaving forever my dear Parents & friends. . . . thine sincerely, D. S. Corse.

To continue with the fortunes and misfortunes of *Furley Hall,* we learn that after 1902 the mansion was no longer in the possession of the Corses, and that it was burned down in 1906 on purpose. A certain man set fire to the pile in order to collect insurance. He was sanguine enough to believe that he could collect insurance twice by the same method: he had already put the torch to *Clairmont* and succeeded in getting cash. But after *Furley* burned, the law caught up with him. The kitchen wing was saved, but the main part of the house and the dining-room portion succumbed. An ugly farm structure was then erected over the old stone basement of the main block, and the dining room cellar was filled in.

Faded old photographs show the appearance of *Furley*. The main part was a two-storey, clapboarded Georgian mansion with hipped roof, brick chimneys, and a front gable with large oculus or bull's eye window. The entrance doorway had a triangular pediment over a semicircular fanlight transom, and Ionic pilasters flanking a six-panel door. The main cornice had modillions and dentils. A similar cornice went up the sides of all the gables, front and rear. At the back or garden side the roof of the main block sloped down lower than on the front; and there was a fourteen-foot-wide porch with Doric columns helping to hold up two bed-rooms at the rear. The columns were round and had octagonal bases upon square plinths. Having every appearance of an addition, the porch itself formed an out-door living room—for even in the eighteenth century men thought about such conveniences. Two porch walls were plastered white and lined with chair rail and baseboard.

Upon entering the front doorway of *Furley*, one came into a passageway about nine feet wide, with an easy-rising stairway on the left side of it. To the right was the sitting room or Back Parlor; to the left, the Best Parlor or Great Room, with its delicately-carved white Directoire mantel that had rinceaux, garlands, urns, oval patterae, and down-tapering pilasters. Flanking the fireplace were semi-circular, round-headed alcoves framed with pilasters on pedestals. Set in separate panels, the French wallpaper was in the Pompeian manner, with arabesques.

Off the northwest side of the main block stood a brick wing in two parts: the dining-room section and the kitchen portion. The former was unusual in that pedimented gables with bull's eyes faced front and rear, resulting in a valley between its roof and the higher wall of the main block. This arrangement must have produced a gusset and perhaps some leaks. But it was no worse a design than the triple gables found in Bermuda or the Bahamas.

The dining-room section, too, was set back two feet from the line of the main block, indicating that it was built at a different time. Nowhere does this chronology appear more evident than in the cornice arrangement of the garden façade, where the main cornice fits awkwardly against the cornice above the dining-room section. At the rear of the dining room was an office, known after 1847 as William Corse's Office or Study, which opened onto the porch. The dining room itself had a fireplace flush with the wall and a deep cupboard large enough to hide a full-grown bear.

In going from the dining room to the little passageway or pantry in the kitchen wing, one descended five steps to a level almost at the ground. The kitchen

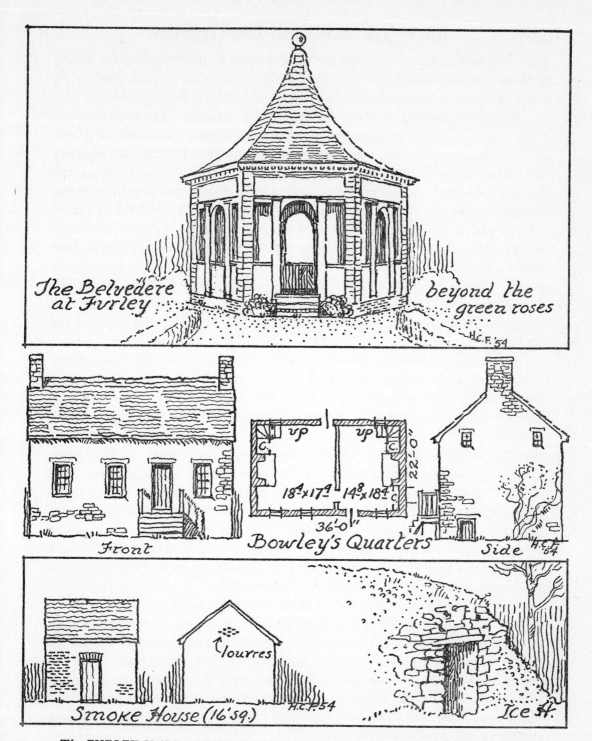

The *Belvedere at Fvrley* ... beyond the green roses

H.C.F. '54

Front

Bowley's Quarters

up   up

C.   C.

$18^4 \times 17^9$ $14^8 \times 18^4$

22'-0"

36'-0"

C.

Side   H.C.F. '54

Smoke House (16' sq.)

lourres

H.C.F. '54

Ice H.

The FURLEY HALL outbuildings, as drawn and reconstructed by the writer, before the bulldozer push of 1953 and complete destruction. Johns Hopkins and Enoch Pratt often frequented the belvedere.

was a capacious one, twenty feet square, and had a fireplace carrying a heavy wood lintel reaching in span seven feet and eight inches. Beside the fireplace was the customary winding staircase, this having seven risers in a ninety-degree turn.

The second floor plan of *Furley* followed in a general way the outlines of the first. The main back stairs ascended from the kitchen passageway to an upstairs passage which opened into the servants' bedroom over the kitchen and, by means of further steps, into the second floor of the dining-room section. By 1953, before the destruction of this part of *Furley*, the upstairs passage was used as a harness room of the riding academy. There were wall hooks for Hopper Pink, Red Cloud, Texas, Belle, Pal Ginger, and Blossom Knockout. The bedroom space over the kitchen had been cut up by two-inch-thick plastered board partitions, which did not fit well into wall and ceiling. Also, the small fireplace had been covered.

Over the dining room and office were other bedrooms. Above the sitting room was a large chamber known as Aunt Carrie Corse's Bedroom, and over the Best Parlor was the Best Bedroom. As you came up the front stairway and reached the level of the landing, you could gain access by means of a step or two steps to two small bedrooms over the porch. The windows of these bedrooms were cross-latticed in order to keep out flying squirrels.

The stone basement, which extended originally under the main block and the dining-room section, had a dirt floor, and over in the northwest corner was a little access door to the subcellar, a wine vault. It is said that this lower cavity was filled in before 1906 because of gaseous odors originating there.

On either side of the front door stood two magnolia grandiflora trees, which had been planted in honor of Deborah Sinclair Corse. About twenty-five feet back of the office stood a magnificent Cedar of Lebanon, already mentioned. Other fine specimens of trees were a purple beech and a Chinese ginkgo. On the axis of the back door and connecting the back porch with a summerhouse or belvedere, was a gravel walk which, about thirty feet from the porch, divided into a circle. It was near this circle that the noted green rosebush bloomed. In her *Green Rose of Furley*,[2] Helen Corse Barney identified the rose as the Rosa Chinensia Viridiflora.

The frame belvedere (pp. 161, 185) was capacious and eight-sided. The roof swallowtailed outward all the way from the finial at the apex to the eaves line. Like that of the main house, the cornice had modillions and a frieze; but there were no dentils. Each of the eight sides had a round-arched doorway flanked by narrow windows, and the corners were rusticated in wood—that is, they imitated stone blocks with deep-set joints. There were no screens in the belvedere. During William Corse's ownership of *Furley*, this summerhouse was a favorite rendezvous of certain Friends, including Enoch Pratt and Johns Hopkins.

[2] Crown Publishers, Inc., New York, 1953.

The long vista of outbuildings which the visitor saw upon bringing his carriage to the front door was an interesting feature of the *Furley* plantation. The plot plan (p. 159) indicates this string of structures. First was the brick smoke house, the door of which had been cut more widely by 1953 for purposes of a stable. It was sixteen feet square and had louvres or small ventilating openings pierced in the gables. For some unknown reason one gable had nine holes, the other only three.

About forty feet beyond the smoke house stood *Bowley's Slave Quarters*, already mentioned in connection with the police dog and the suspicious tenant. It was a cottage of field stone, one and a half storeys high, with basement (p. 161). This was believed to have been the first Bowly home on the estate, and to have been constructed in the late seventeenth century. But proof is lacking for both beliefs. At any rate, we do know that the Bowlys gave the name to Bowley's Lane, Bowley's Quarter, Bowley's Bar—a sand bank, not a "hot" spot—and Bowley's Wharf. But Daniel Bowly, the immigrant from Gloucestershire, did not construct *Bowley's Quarters*, because he was not born until 1715. There is a fancy story, at the ghost level, that he was kidnaped by pirates in England and was taken to the West Indies. It is possible that he and his family lived in *Bowley's Quarters* cottage before the mansion, *Furley Hall*, was built. These *Quarters* measured thirty-six feet long by twenty-two feet wide and had the typical early plan of the hall-and-parlor variety. The two bedrooms had sloping ceilings and lie-on-your-stomach windows. By 1953 *Bowley's Quarters* was so heavily encrusted with ivy that it was almost impossible to take measurements. And on the interior was the ugly-tempered police dog—at least in the last few days.

Further on down the lane stood the large stone barn (p. 155), measuring seventy-five and a half feet by thirty. The crew running the bulldozers boasted to this writer that they could level this stone pile in one hour. The walls were two feet thick, and the gables had loopholes. In 1914, the interior had burned out, but it was later replaced.

The spring house in 1953 had become so surrounded with snake-infested vegetation that it was impossible to obtain much of a view of it. In the garden formerly had stood a necessary house. Down the slope at the southwest end of the mansion stood an egg-shaped subterranean ice house, built of rock, choked with myrtle and ivy, and shaded by tamarack trees. In springtime the lawn about this ice house was sprinkled with bluebells and daffodils.

Among the outbuildings which had vanished without a trace by 1953 was a small stone bathhouse with a tub and a stove, which had stood near the spring house. During the Civil War when it became unsafe to walk to school, classes were held in the bathhouse and presided over by Aunt Hetty, a member of the Corse family.

2. SCOTT PLANTATIONS IN BALTIMORE
COUNTY

BY WAY OF introduction to Baltimore County antiquities, may we point out that the stonework and some of the thoroughfares are of interest.

There are five principal kinds of stone. First is marble, which is found largely about Cockeysville and Texas, Maryland. The dominant variety of marble is dolomite, which was used in 1815 in the Washington Monument, Baltimore. At that time the cost of masonry called "Circular marble ashler rubbed on the face," from Scott's Quarry on Western Run, was $1.90 a foot, that is, a solid stone twelve inches deep and twelve long. The old Beaver Dam marble quarry, near Cockeysville, now full of water, once furnished 108 large columns for the Capitol at Washington, the Washington Monument there, and the Peabody Institute in Baltimore.

The other chief varieties of building stone are the gneiss, which in the trade is called "rust rock," from Jones Falls and Gwynn Falls; flagstone, a thin-bedded quartzite which cleaves into neat, parallel-sided slabs from one to six inches thick, found at Butler and near Loch Raven; granite, common on the Old Court Road near Woodstock; and limestone, no longer quarried.

Baltimore County is fortunate in having preserved the names of many of its early roads. We list some of the most unusual, although lists can be monotonous: Johnnycake Road, named for Johnnycake Town, or Tavern, where in the old days johnnycake with melted butter was served for breakfast; Quaker Bottom Road No. 1; Quaker Bottom Road No. 2; Dance Mill Road; Paper Mill Road; Trump Mill Road—showing how plentiful were the mills of this county. Then there were: Old Court Road, which of course led to the courthouse; Joppa Road, an old Indian trail leading to the little town of Joppa; Satyr Hill Road; Sweathouse Road; Golden Ring Road; Copper Factory Road; Nectar Road; and Garrison Forest Road, leading to the oldest existing fort in the State. Other curiosities are Cold Bottom Road; Yeoho Road; Tan Yard Road, which led past Scott's Tan Yard, mentioned below; Dark Hollow Road; Delight Road; Gunpowder Road; Slab Bridge Road; Frog Hollow Road; Bee Tree Road; Old Nunnery Lane; Putty Hill Avenue; Sweet Air Road; Cinder Road; Broadway; and Spooks Hill Road. When one finds on the map Bread and Cheese Creek, a road by the same name can be expected.

Coming now to the subject of old Scott family plantations in Baltimore County, we find the chief seat located in the pretty Western Run valley, a few miles north of the city of Baltimore. This is *Pleasant Prospect,* or *The Tan Yard*

Farm. This property was part of the Pleasant Prospect tract, which was originally patented by Griffiths. About 1765 the land was purchased by Abraham Scott, Jr., who likewise owned an adjacent farm by the name of *Regulation,* where a mansion, *Rosedale,* was erected later.

The Scotts were members of the Religious Society of Friends and came from England to Maryland by way of Pennsylvania. Robert Scott, of Woodhall, Cumberland, England, in 1657 married Mary Hamond at the Holme Friends' Meetinghouse. In 1687 their son, John Scott, married Elizabeth Cupe. It was John and Elizabeth Scott's child, Abraham Scott, Sr., who brought his Quaker certificate of removal (1722) from Woodhall meeting in Britain to the Gunpowder Friends' Meeting in Baltimore County, Maryland. Abraham in 1726 married Elizabeth Dyer of Philadelphia, and had Abraham Scott, Jr., who became owner of the Pleasant Prospect and Regulation tracts.

It appears that about 1765 Abraham, Jr., erected a temporary shelter, a log cabin, on *Pleasant Prospect,* and lived there with his wife, the former Elizabeth Rossiter, a lady from Wales whom he had married in 1751. He is believed to have erected the original portion of the *Scott's Mill House* about 1770.

The simple cabin was not ample enough for this growing family of plain tastes, so the existing stone dwelling, *Pleasant Prospect,* was erected in 1824 by Jesse Scott, son of Abraham Scott, Jr., and his wife Elizabeth. The stonework of the front and the gables is excellent limestone masonry, of which we present a detail (p. 186) as a good sample of early nineteenth-century work. On a trip to this house in 1938 or 1939, this writer had the pleasure of escorting the president of Goucher College to show him this fine example of Baltimore County stonework as preparatory study for the new Towson campus buildings of that college.

At the rear of *Pleasant Prospect* homestead the wall is built of coarser stuff —the typical brown field stone, gneiss, of this region.

After serving for about sixty-six years, the log cabin, which adjoined the 1824 house already described, was taken down (1838), and in its stead a new stone kitchen room was constructed. This wing still stands, and possesses two fireplaces each facing the other, one of them a remnant of the log building. To complete the history of this plantation house, we should mention the modern wing of 1939-40 which was added to the west gable.

Especially interesting today is the fact that *Pleasant Prospect* was a self-economic unit in the truest sense of the word. In the early days it was a long journey from this farm to Baltimore City, and one could not drive by automobile to the department stores on Howard Street in a few minutes. So the Scotts made most of the things which they needed right on their home place. The lane known as the Tan Yard Road still runs through *Pleasant Prospect* and gave it an alternate

EARLY SCOTT BUILDINGS IN BALTIMORE COUNTY

*A drawing copied by the writer from a faded photograph of not later
than 1879. The scene is in the Western Run valley.*

← To Scott's Mill barn   Rosedale barn   Rosedale 1806

Wagon Shed   Scott's Mill House   Wood Shed
Ice House   1842 c.1770 c.1820
Mill Race   (original)

Pleasant Prospect barn & corn crib	Vat H. (left) Finishing H. & Bark H. (rt.)	Pleasant Prospect House 1824 1838	Spring H. 1830
Hebron Mill c.1770	Scott's Mill Spring H.		

name, *Scott's Tan Yard*. Operated by three generations of Scotts—Jesse, Abraham III, who was the son of Jesse, and Edwin, son of Abraham III, from about 1800 to 1885—the tannery comprised three stone structures on the edge of the Yard. In 1951 two of these buildings still survived: the Vat House, about twenty-two feet by twenty-eight, and the Drying or Finishing or Currying House, about eighteen feet by twenty-two. The third, long since gone, was the Bark House, about twenty-two by forty-four feet.

The principal process of tanning took place not indoors but in the Yard, where tannic acid was applied to the hides lying in the vats. There formerly stood long parallel lines of vats, which have now disappeared. The Vat House was filled with lime vats employed to remove the hair from the hides. Then the Currying House was for the purpose of oiling and rolling the leather after it came out of the vats. As the name indicates, the Bark House was used to store bark and to keep it dry so that it would grind easily. There the grinder was kept. Inside, a blind horse—no good for anything else—used to go around in circles, grinding the bark to powder.

On *Pleasant Prospect* there are other outbuildings: the barn (p. 187), the corn house, the smoke house, the spring house—all substantially built of stone. An oven, separate from the dwelling and located next to the smoke house, has been destroyed. On the spring house are a carved date and initials, "1830 ARS," the letters standing for Abraham Scott III and his wife Rachel. In the same manner the stone kitchen wing has the date "1838" and "AS" for Abraham III.

But the Tan Yard was not enough of an occupation for this energetic family which helped to make our country a leader in the world. The Scotts also operated a quarry and a mill. As has been already indicated, the Washington Monument, designed in 1814 in Baltimore by Robert Mills, architect, was mostly built from Scott marble. In the articles of agreement dated December 20, 1815, between Owner and Contractors, it is stated: "The whole of the Column is to be of the whitest and best quality Marble from Scott's quarry."

Scott's Mill, located above this quarry, was known as *Hebron Mills*, built about 1770 on the plantation *Regulation*, adjoining *Pleasant Prospect*. The mill shows in our drawing of Early Scott Buildings (p. 167), but unfortunately about 1878 it was burned. Nevertheless, the stone *Mill House* or miller's habitat remains. It is believed that Abraham Scott, Jr., builder of the original Scott log cabin, erected both *Hebron Mills* and *Scott's Mill House* for his son, Thomas Scott.

Although constructed about 1770, a little before the American Revolutionary War, the original section of this mill dwelling is an excellent example of the persistence, or Hangover, of the Medieval Style of architecture into the eighteenth century. This portion stood in the center; the east wing (c. 1820) has been de-

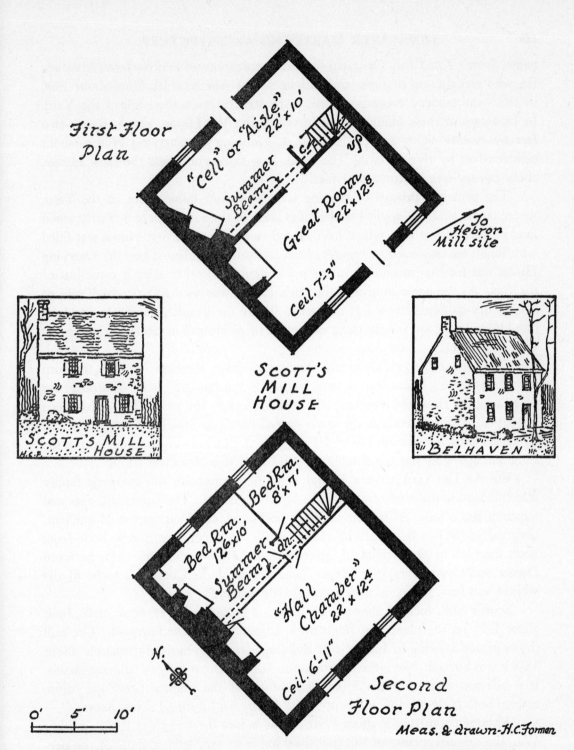

First Floor Plan

"Cell" or "Aisle" 22' x 10'

Summer Beam

Great Room 22' x 12.8

Ceil. 7'-3"

To Hebron Mill site

SCOTT'S MILL HOUSE

SCOTT'S MILL HOUSE
H.C.F.

BELHAVEN

Bed Rm. 12.6 x 10'

Bed Rm. 8' x 7'

Summer Beam

dn.

"Hall Chamber" 22' x 12.4

Ceil. 6'-11"

N

Second Floor Plan

Meas. & drawn - H. C. Forman

0' 5' 10'

Floor plans and front elevation of the original section (c.1770) of SCOTT'S MILL HOUSE, built in the Hangover Medieval Style by Abraham Scott, Jr. On right is BELHAVEN, an old Mason homestead of about 1780-90.

stroyed; and the west or largest portion, with its horseshoe stair, was erected in 1842 by "TES," Thomas E. Scott. When the house was complete in 1842, it formed a telescope with the original miller's dwelling in the center.

Now, this middle or earliest part (p. 169) is square, two storeys and attic high, built of brown field stone, and has on first and second floors great summer beams. A boxed, break-your-neck staircase rises from the Great Room or Hall to a tiny upstairs passage which opens onto three bedrooms. Not the least interesting are the two catercornered fireplaces, on different floor levels, and the two-inch-thick partitions comprising random-width, vertical boards on one side and plaster on the other.

When this writer in the dead of winter of 1951-52 visited this mill-house property and drove his car across a slippery field having the attributes of glue, he found, after an absence of thirteen years, that the atmosphere of chill wind sweeping through the broken window panes and across the refuse and rags of the interior had formed a picture not soon to be forgotten. Fortunately the dwelling now has new owners and has been renovated.

The plantation *Regulation* also included *Rosedale*, another Scott home, which, like the mill house, was erected in three sections. The earliest or west end was constructed in 1806 by Jesse Scott and has the inscription "IRS 1806" for Jesse and Rebecca Scott. The middle section was put up by Jesse's son, Abraham III, of whom we have already made note. Latest in date is the kitchen wing. The whole of *Rosedale* forms an ample, typical dwelling in the Hangover Georgian manner. In the early days the building is said to have served as a store. The walls are a curious mixture of limestone and field stone, the latter forming patches on the surface. At one side of *Rosedale* are two stone outbuildings, a smoke house, with outside stairway, and a spring-and-wash house, access to which is had by a footbridge across a stream. In the yard are millstones believed to have been brought from France—a belief held in spite of Scott's mill having been on the same property. The millstones are of pieced stones bound together with iron bands.

In the little printed booklet, *Golden Wedding, Mr. and Mrs. John Scott, 1827-1877*, it is stated that "This deed of the old homestead [*Regulation*] to Abraham Scott [Jr.], your grandfather, is dated October 18, 1786, and May 15, 1787."

3. *MASON'S FOLLY* OR *BELHAVEN*

OF THE SCOTT family of *Pleasant Prospect*, Baltimore County, Rachel Scott, daughter of Abraham Scott, Jr. and his wife, Elizabeth Rossiter, by her father's will in 1799 inherited 100 acres of land, part of a tract called *Belhaven*. This property later received the nicknames of *Mason's Folly* and *Pear Hill*.

Continuing with the genealogy of this noted Quaker family, we find that on March 2, 1780, Rachel Scott married James Mason, according to the Gunpowder Monthly Meeting Certificate on record at Stony Run, Baltimore. She died in 1837, and her will is recorded in the Baltimore City Court House. Her husband, James Mason, was the son of George Mason and Jane his wife, who in 1767 joined the Gunpowder Friends' Meeting "with some lines of Recommendation from Friends in Old England showing Friends Unity with him in the Ministry."

The *Belhaven* dwelling, built by James Mason probably soon after his marriage in 1780, is plain, square, and stone (p. 169). Its walls form a pleasant contrast of limestone and brown field stone. Its two storeys and attic stand four-square upon the pleasant meadow land. The east wing, which has been torn down in recent years, had a stone inscription, "J M 1855," which has now been set in a modern wall.

The great front door at *Belhaven* had a stock lock escutcheon of ornamental shape with a brass handle. There was place to put a finger or two when opening the door (p. 188). The lock has now disappeared.

The will of Abraham Scott, Jr., gave to his daughter Rachel 100 acres, part of *Belhaven*, but there was a provision that after her death the property was to be divided equally between her two daughters, Elizabeth and Rachel Mason.

Of these two girls, Elizabeth Mason married Isaac Kinsey. Their daughter, Rachel Mason Kinsey, was born in 1805 and married Gardner Betterton (1797-1833) of Baltimore, formerly of Philadelphia, Pennsylvania. And their daughter was Elizabeth Betterton, of *The Turner Family of Hebron and Betterton, Maryland*, a little work by this writer. It is interesting that when Rachel Mason Kinsey was fourteen years of age (that is, in 1819), she sewed a fine sampler (p. 185), twenty-one inches long, showing a shepherd and his dog under a tree, with a wattled and thatched cabin in the background. We like to think, as we dine almost every day beside this work of art, that it is a representation of the Good Shepherd.

4. THE FRIENDS' MEETINGHOUSE OF
OLD GUNPOWDER

FAR UP IN THE hills back of Towson, Baltimore County, and at the present moment being engulfed by a modern ranch house real estate development, *Old Gunpowder Friends' Meetinghouse* stands forlorn and neglected. In recent years this house of worship has deteriorated, and now, with entire sash windows smashed in and with animals walking in and out the doorways at will, complete destruction is to be expected. When the roof goes, the building goes.

Owned by Stony Run Friends' Meeting in Baltimore, *Old Gunpowder*, built in 1773, is the finest example of the persistence of Medieval Style into the eighteenth century in Baltimore County, and one of the half dozen best examples in the State.[1] But is it necessary to declare that because of its architectural significance this fane needs and merits preservation? We foretell that county, state, and nation, as well as the Religious Society of Friends themselves, will within the next half century regret the destruction of this shrine. How shortsighted can we be? What happened to the home of Wenlocke Christison, Maryland's foremost pioneer of religious freedom?

With more and more Quakers moving out of the City of Baltimore to make homes in the County, there must be some who would be interested in the upkeep of this meetinghouse and in worshipping there. But will they win the race with the elements—the rain, snow, and hail that now enter its walls?

There is a tradition that the origin of this meeting place came about by the worship of one person seated on a log. He was later joined by other worshippers. There seems to be nothing unusual about this type of religious worship. A year or two ago this writer was called to Dutchess County, New York, to make a reconstruction report on an old Quaker meetinghouse. During that visit he was shown a great estate, *Thorndale*, where the owner, a Friend, believed that the way to get close to God was to sit out in a field on his place by himself rather than to sit with a congregation.

At any rate, at *Old Gunpowder* a log meetinghouse was first erected, and in 1773 rose the present stone building (p. 188). It must have been in the log house that the first marriage was held in 1740, when Samuel Hopkins took Sarah Giles to be his wife. A story, without a date, is told of a courtship taking place at *Old Gunpowder*. John Price and Polly Johnson rode side by side on horseback to meeting on First Day, that is, Sunday. As they were crossing a swollen stream, they stopped in the middle, and he said, "Polly, I'm not going to move from this brook unless thou promisest to be my wife." To which she answered, "John, thou now hast the advantage of me. I guess I'll have to say yes."

In the graveyard behind the meetinghouse, surrounded by a stone wall, there survive a few old stones of the Mathews and Scott families.[2]

The building itself is two and a half storeys high and measures forty feet by

[1] *The Architecture of the Old South*, p. 157.
[2] Oliver Mathews, b. 11th mo. 28, 1721, d. 1st mo. 17, 1824; Elizabeth Scott, d. 8th mo. 20, 1852, aged 83; Thomas Scott, d. 1852, aged 81; R. S., d. 1832; I. S., d. 1843; J. J. P., d. 1841.

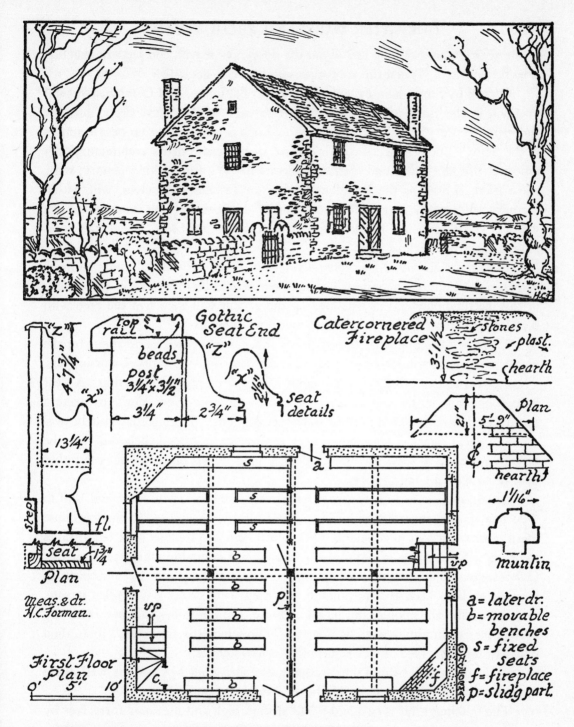

Labels within the illustration:

Gothic Seat End

"Z"
top rail
beads
post 3¼" x 3½"
"Z"
"X"
seat details
3¼" 2¾" 2½"

4-7¾"
"X"
13¼"
seat Plan 1¾"
step fl.

Meas. & dr.
H. C. Forman.

First Floor Plan
0' 5' 10'

Catercornered Fireplace
stones
plast.
hearth
3-1½"
21" 5'-9"
Plan
hearth
1⅛6"
muntin

a = later dr.
b = movable benches
S = fixed seats
f = fireplace
P = slid'g part.

Well on the way to ruin is OLD GUNPOWDER FRIENDS' MEETING (1773), here shown by the writer by floor plan, details, and perspective. Note the two chambers each divided by summer beams into four equal compartments.

twenty. Unfortunately the brown field-stone walls have been crudely repointed. The roof formerly had good cedar shingles, three feet long, before they were burned in the fire of 1886. A certain naïveté is given to the exterior appearance by the two brick corner chimney stacks diametrically opposite each other.

As is customary in old Quaker meetinghouses, there are two doors on the front, each giving upon a square meeting room. Between these two rooms are panelled sliding partitions, to be raised when business meetings are held separately by the men and the women. This old custom of separate business gatherings has now been abandoned in Friends' meeting places.

In one corner of the east room is a shallow, arched fireplace with a brick hearth. In the west room a little boxed, winding staircase formerly led to the second floor but is now blocked. The batten door at the bottom of this stair is only four feet and ten inches high—tall enough for children—and compares favorably with the four-foot door at *Anderton* in Talbot County. In another corner, next to the fixed seats, marked "S" on the floor plan (p. 173), is a diagonal stone and plastered foundation, supposedly for an upstairs fireplace which is now gone.

Besides the batten door and tiny winding staircase—in themselves hangovers from the Middle Ages—the great summer beams and posts carved with lamb's tongues give the strongest medieval flavor. It is true that all the posts have been replaced, with crudely enlarged lamb's tongues and chamfered edges. Also the summer beams, dividing the ceiling of each room into four equal compartments, have been encased with modern boards. Standing upon a raised platform having two steps are two rows of fixed pine seats, pegged together, having their ends carved with Gothic ogee arch profiles. On the floor itself are simple, movable pine benches, most of which have disappeared.

The windows and doors have quarter-round moldings on their frames and are pegged together. The shutters are paneled, some possessing strap hinges with heart-shaped terminations and others H-hinges. The sash have wide muntins and are two panes high, but four wide. We found one glass bubble two and a half inches long.

Supported by great strap hinges, the exterior doors have diagonal boards backed by vertical boards inside. There are thumb latches, great iron-rim locks, and wooden bars which can be slipped into wrought-iron fasteners on the door frames, in the manner of old castle-doorway bars. Lest anyone think he could strip this meetinghouse with impunity, let him remember that he would be under an eternal curse for robbing a house of God.

The interior walls are wainscoted with random-width, beaded, vertical boards to a level just above the window sills. On the rear or north wall one can look up into a pocket inside a window and see the irregular, uncut line of second-floor boards sticking out—one of the curious features of *Old Gunpowder*. The outside doorway on the north may have been originally a window and designed for ventilation.

In addition to the winding staircase, access was had to the upper floor, where formerly guests were lodged at the time of yearly meetings, by a stairway entered from the outside through a doorway in the east wall. So changed and ruined is the upstairs that it is difficult to trace the original room arrangement. There is a summer beam on the longitudinal axis of the structure which is supported in the middle by a post, located exactly over the largest king post downstairs. Probably there was a solid partition just over the sliding partition below, thus dividing the second floor into two equal guest chambers. The west room evidently had a catercornered fireplace which has been removed or concealed. Traces of a former stepladder to the loft may still be seen in the east room. Gazing up through this black hole in the ceiling, one can dimly make out that the rafters and collar beams are pegged—probably a construction after the fire of 1886.

We should not take leave of this ancient structure without making a note that it is called *Old Gunpowder* in contradistinction to the *New Gunpowder Meeting-house*, erected in 1821 on a hilltop several miles to the north.

5. *THE TOWN HOUSE OF MARY PICKERSGILL,* AND HER FLAG

ONE OF THE most noted public buildings in the City of Baltimore is Mrs. Mary Young Pickersgill's town house (p. 195), built in 1793 at the corner of Pratt Street and Albemarle. Now known as *The Star-Spangled Banner Flag House*, or *Flag House* for short, it forms a handsome and typical example of the kind of urban row-dwelling erected near the Baltimore waterfront toward the close of the eighteenth century. In style it is Hangover Georgian with some Federal details.

The premises seem to be steeped in flag-making history. Mrs. Mary Pickersgill, whose mother, Rebecca Young, had made the first flag of the American Revolution—the Cambridge or Grand Union flag,—was chosen in the year 1813 to make a large banner which was to fly over Fort McHenry in expectation of an attack by ships of the British fleet. At that time Major George Armistead was in charge of this Fort, and upon his request General John S. Stricker and Commodore Joshua Barney went to the two-and-a-half-storey brick house on Pratt Street where Mrs. Pickersgill lived, and commissioned her to make a flag. This ensign was forty-two feet long and thirty feet high, conforming to the wish of Major Armistead that it must be so large that the enemy would have no difficulty in seeing it a long way off. Following the terms of a resolution of 1794 by the United States Congress, the Pickersgill flag had fifteen stripes and fifteen stars. It is now on exhibit in the Smithsonian Institution in Washington.

But it was not the fact that Mary Pickersgill sewed the stars and stripes together which makes that ensign so noted. It was the completed banner which flew at the mast over Fort McHenry during the fierce bombardment by the British on September 13 and 14, 1814, which inspired Francis Scott Key to write *The Star-Spangled Banner*, a poem which is now enshrined in the Maryland Historical Society, Baltimore. This poem became our national anthem.

In 1927, one hundred thirty-four years after it was built, Mary Pickersgill's home was purchased by the City and was put in the charge of the Star-Spangled Banner Flag Association, Incorporated.

Originally the domicile was one room wide and two rooms deep, and there existed a separate kitchen structure at the rear. A narrow passageway on the first floor, measuring only six feet wide, was divided in the middle by an archway, which has now disappeared, but which is shown in the floor plan (p. 178). The back part of the passageway is occupied by a stairway, the newel of which is of interest, though very typical. This newel post has a square base and cap, and the shaft is rounded. The cap is topped by a circular button. Repeating the motifs of newel and handrail along the wall are half-newel posts and chair rail. There are no spandrels or decorative step ends, and there is a closed string—that is, the steps are closed off by a board. Under this stairway are steep steps leading down to a cellar which was at first merely a hole in the ground.

Upstairs there is a front bedchamber with handsome cupboard doors next to a manteled fireplace, and a back bedroom, also with a fireplace. On the third or attic floor there was at first only one large room.

The attic staircase inconveniently—let us emphasize, very inconveniently—permits a head room under the sloping-ceiling of only thirty-one inches at the *middle* of the top step. Even pigmies could not ascend the middle of this stair without knocking their heads. After the dwelling was built, this attic stair was acknowledged by the owners to be impossible, for another piece of staircase, of five risers, was built branching off from it. It is true that this new section of steps has improved head room, but only enough for a person five-foot-two-inches tall.

Probably in the first quarter of the nineteenth century a brick kitchen ell was added to the house and rose to the same height—two storeys and attic. This addition enlarged the habitation by a more convenient cooking room and two bedrooms.

· RECONSTRUCTION · OF · FLAG · HOUSE · FAÇADE · 1793 ·
WRENN, LEWIS & JENCKS, A.I.A., ARCHITECTS · HENRY CHANDLEE FORMAN, A.I.A., ASSOCIATE

"One of the most noted public buildings in the City of Baltimore is MRS. MARY YOUNG PICKERSGILL'S TOWN HOUSE. In style it is Hangover Georgian with some Federal details."

The appearance of the main façade of the *Flag House* involved a bit of research—first, the examining of the brickwork; second, the finding of an old photograph of 1907 (p. 194) which shows a late nineteenth-century bay window with sheets of plate glass. By the time of the 1953 reconstruction of the front, of which we show the preliminary sketch (p. 177), this little bay had been replaced with a large plate-glass window flush with the wall, and the front door had been moved over to the other side of this window. The original pilastered doorway had vanished. The frieze, cornice, sunken oval patterae, and transom of this old doorway, shown dimly in the 1907 photograph, formed a good example of Federal or Early Republican wood carving.

In 1955 further repairs and renovations were made to the *Flag House*, including cleaning and repointing of the brick on the Albemarle Street side. It is an understatement to remark that this fine old brickwork has been badly repointed by covering up the edges of the brick, consequently making the mortar joints too wide and giving an inaccurately restored appearance and texture. This type of workmanship was aptly described in *Early Manor and Plantation Houses of Maryland* under the heading, "So-called Improvements." A good restoration necessitates a good specialist and qualified supervision.

In 1953 the *Flag House Museum Building* was erected in the rear of the *Flag House* over the site of where by tradition stood the old kitchen (p. 179). In this structure, built to conform with the style of the dwelling to which it is appended by a colonnade, are kept relics concerning the Pickersgills and the Star-Spangled Banner and the *Town House* which is the subject of this sketch.

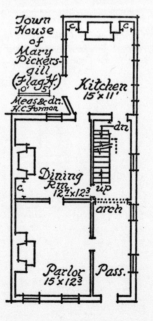

THE FLAG HOUSE MUSEUM BUILDING
WRENN, LEWIS, AND JENCKS, A.I.A., ARCHITECTS
HENRY CHANDLEE FORMAN A.I.A. ASSOCIATE

Nov. 3 '52

The MUSEUM BUILDING, connected to the Flag House by a colonnade, was erected on the site of the original kitchen house, and holds the Star-Spangled Banner relics.

An old, faded photograph of the approach front of FURLEY HALL, in the City of Baltimore, before the fire of 1906. Note the bull's eye with square, Victorian window in the pediment.

The porch at FURLEY HALL, Baltimore, formed a comfortable, outdoor living area, framed by Doric Columns on octagonal bases. Notice the plastered walls, chair rail, and baseboard.

William Corse, Sr. (1804-1869), after 1847 the owner of FURLEY HALL.

Deborah Sinclair Corse (1810-1899), who grew up at CLAIRMONT, near FURLEY HALL.

The Great Room, or "Best Parlor," in FURLEY HALL, had a delicately-carved Directoire mantel, and French wallpaper in the Pompeiian manner. Late Georgian elegance in Baltimore.

In the garden at FURLEY HALL stand, left to right, Deborah Sinclair Corse, "Aunt" Carrie Corse, Samuel Register, a neighbor, and Frank E. Corse. Below, the sampler of a shepherd and his dog sewn in 1819 by Rachel Mason Kinsey, of BELHAVEN or MASON'S FOLLY.

A good example of dressed limestone masonry in the first quarter of the 19th century is here seen at the PLEASANT PROSPECT HOUSE, a home of the Scott and Bosley families, in Baltimore County. Author, 1939.

Hidden away from the country road stands small telescopic CUMBERLAND, illustrating how the early builder could create charm by a few simple planes and masses. Author, 1954.

The stone barn at PLEASANT PROSPECT, Baltimore County, has "hourglass" lou-vres made of brick in a decorative pattern. On right are Vat House, Drying House, and the mansion. Below, the MATHEWS-TIPTON PLACE, Baltimore County, the first part of which was the log cabin. Author, 1939.

The stock-lock, wrought-iron escutcheon with brass handle, which formerly stood on the great front door of BEL-HAVEN, home of James Mason. Author, 1940.

Below, the front façade of the OLD GUNPOWDER FRIENDS' MEETINGHOUSE, built in 1773 in Baltimore County, with the writer's son, Richard Townsend T., on the doorstep. The two doors led to rooms separated by movable partitions. Author, 1939.

The "Hangover" Medieval interior of the OLD GUNPOWDER FRIENDS' MEET-
INGHOUSE (1773). Below, GARDEN OF EDEN, an old Wilson home, has a main
block dating from the 18th century, and the 19th; with low-ceiled kitchen "outshut"
at the rear. Author, 1939.

A map of 1706 identifies this plantation in Baltimore County as PORK FOREST, but the name has never been explained. The stone dwelling is reputed to have been erected in 1787. The classic garden, and gazebo or summerhouse, were designed by the present owner. Scarff.

The kitchen wing and milk house at PERRY HALL, Talbot County. Of English bond, the kitchen forms part of the first dwelling. Author, 1934. Below are the frame garden tool house and the brick ash house, of the 1830s, at BURLEY MANOR, Worcester County. Author, 1954.

Hip-roof Georgian in ecclesiastical architecture. Known as OLD HERRING CREEK, ST. JAMES EPISCOPAL CHURCH (1763), Anne Arundel County, has a side porch in English fashion. Two walls of the church have "All-header" bond, the others English. Inside, a plaster barrel-vault, coved under the hips. Author, 1954.

A detail of the wall of the derelict END-ING OF CONTROVERSIE house (c 1670), Talbot County. Post-and-beam construction covered by random-width vertical boards and battens. Author, 1935.

A detail of the collapsed brick gable-end at THE ENDING OF CONTROVERSIE, having a kind of palisade wall construction. Note the top of the staircase to the bedroom shown in the drawing on p. (73). Author, 1935.

Above, *a view of part of an important building in Baltimore, showing how* not *to re-point old brickwork. Note 20th-century vining and too-wide joints. Below, preview of the next book of this series: Maryland wattles and half-timber work will be described. Author.*

APPENDIX

THE *KENT FORT MANOR* AND *ST. PETER'S KEY* MYTHS[1]

In the light of further study and new material at hand, the time has come when certain misconceptions about two of the so-called oldest houses in Maryland should be corrected. Both these buildings were found by the writer on field trips in the year 1932. They are now known as *Kent Fort Manor*, on Kent Island, and *St. Peter's Key*, in St. Mary's City.

If you travel south on Kent Island, you will come eventually to a sign on a gate painted in ornamental lettering announcing "Kent Fort Manor" and the owner's name.

The 1940 W. P. A.'s *Maryland, A Guide to the Old Line State*—hereinafter referred to as the *Guide*—on page 419 gives directions to Kent Fort Manor and a short description, the gist of which relates that the house was built between 1638 and 1640, that it is of modest size, of brick and weatherboarding, that the hallway has vertical paneling, and that the stairway has less than five feet of head room. The major part of this description was taken from the writer's *Early Manor and Plantation Houses of Maryland*,[2] the first publication to take note of this little dwelling. This volume has photographs of the exterior, showing the plain appearance of the building, and of the interior, with the low-clearance stairway. There is a measured floor plan giving the exact size and arrangement of the structure. The text declares that date to be "probably 1638-40," which later became in the *Guide* "between 1638 and 1640." The Appendix in *Early Manors* purports to show why Kent Fort Manor is probably the oldest known house in Maryland. Fortunately this questionable and now outworn argument was placed in an appendix.

[1] Reprinted, with changes, from the *Maryland Historical Magazine*, vol. xlix, no. 2, June, 1954.
[2] (Easton, 1934), pp. 202, 245-246.

As is often the case, the *Guide* borrowed material which was wrong in the book from which it was taken. This dwelling has never been, is not now, and never will be, the original Kent Fort Manor. It is but an old house on the lands of Kent Fort Manor; it never should have a bronze plaque on account of its age.

Study of the moldings and other details of this building since the publication of *Early Manors* proves its erection after 1800. It is true that the place possesses medieval characteristics, such as brick nogging, vertical paneling, and tiny doorway. Nonetheless, such features in this abode are stylish hangovers into the nineteenth century. Further, the stair is an open well stairway, not a closed-box staircase which is usually found in small homes of the seventeenth century. The small bead molding on the hall paneling, easily distinguished in the photograph in *Early Manors*, is a nineteenth-century feature. For characteristic moldings in vertical-board paneling of earliest Maryland, the reader is referred to the Great Room wainscoting of Old Bloomfield and The Ending of Controversie on the Eastern Shore.

Besides, the common bond of the exposed chimney face and the transom over the main west door are indications of late construction.

Consequently, the existing cabin labeled "Kent Fort Manor" is no more Kent Fort Manor than any other structure on the southern end of Kent Island within the bounds of the manorial grant. The original manor house has been destroyed.

The other house is the so-called St. Peter's Key, located within the original town limits of St. Mary's City. The W. P. A. *Guide* on page 481 informs the reader how to reach this dwelling and assigns to it a paragraph, the essence of which describes that it was named for the key-shaped creek beside which it stands, that it has a free-standing double chimney with pent and a cellar which were erected "about 1650." The *Guide* goes on to relate that the property was patented in 1640 to John Harris and Thomas Allen, and then notes how it came into possession of one Roger Oliver, who was slain in 1643 by an Indian aboard a vessel. Oliver's widow, Blanche Harrison Oliver, who inherited the property, did wilful perjury, and as a result, had both her ears amputated. The *Guide* continues that the Oliver family's "ignominy" persisted in a law decree that the mark of their cattle should be a left ear cropped and, in the right ear, two slits.

Now, all this material was taken in its entirety, but somewhat garbled and without any acknowledgment or reference even in the bibliographical list, from this writer's copyrighted *Jamestown and St. Mary's: Buried Cities of Romance* (Johns Hopkins Press, 1938), which on pages 302 to 304, gives a full description of this house, in part as follows:

". . . standing intact in the city is St. Peter's Key . . . named after the St. Peter's Key Creek on whose green banks it lies. . . . Its chimney-pent closet between free-standing chimneys, its steep roof and gray gables . . . preserve the spirit of old St. Mary's more than anything else in the whole countryside. . . . On the 6th of June, 1640, Governor Leonard Calvert requested his surveyor to lay out fifty acres of land . . . for John Harris and Thomas Allen. . . ."

Next in *Jamestown and St. Mary's* is described the bloody fight which Roger Oliver, owner of St. Peter's Key, in 1643 had with an Indian in the hold of a ship. The story is based on an account in the *Archives of Maryland*:

"Thus, on a day in 1643, Roger Oliver, mariner, left St. Peter's Key to his widow and two children. Five years later an added misfortune struck this family. The widow, Blanche Harrison Oliver, wedded to Humphrey Howell, was condemned, according to English law, to stand in the pillory and lose both her ears, because of wilful perjury. According to the records, the sentence was executed at once. The two Oliver children were assigned their mother's two cows and heifer, and also a cow due her from the Lord Proprietary. . . . Ironically, the mark for their cattle was decreed by law to be: left ear cropt and two slits in the right ear on the underside."

Parenthetically it may be observed that the cropping and slitting of cattle ears was the widespread custom in those days, and that the "ignominy" cited in the *Guide* is a figment of the imagination.

There then follows an architectural description of this house noting that the earliest portion was built "probably about 1645 or 1650," dates which in the *Guide* (p. 123) become for the whole dwelling "1650," and again (p. 481) "about 1650." The phrase, "in the city," becomes (p. 123) "near St. Mary's City."

Further research since *Jamestown and St. Mary's* appeared in 1938 has disclosed that the St. Peter's Key land in this city which James Walter Thomas marked on a map of the town in his *Chronicles of Colonial Maryland* (1913) was not the same property, which in fact was located a goodly distance away. The exact site of the original St. Peter's Key tract will be shown in a forthcoming study of the first capital of Maryland.

The *Guide* borrowed material which was wrong in the source from which it was taken: the aforementioned structure has never been, is not now, and never will be the original St. Peter's Key. The tale of Oliver's fight with the Indian is true enough—if the *Archives* are true—but that event had to do with the owner of a house in St. Mary's City long ago destroyed.

The local name of the existing dwelling labeled "St. Peter's Key" is the Leigh House, named for members of the Leigh family who owned large tracts of land in St. Mary's City in the eighteenth century. Until further research discloses its original name, the "Leigh House" will have to serve. The land on which it stands comprises St. Mary's Hill Freehold, which was first granted in 1639 to Ferdinand

Poulton and which later came into the possession of Major Nicholas Sewall, stepson of Charles Calvert, third Lord Baltimore.

In conclusion this writer wishes to protest the unfortunate fate of the Leigh House. But first, let us go back to 1937 when *Jamestown and St. Mary's* was being written. While the ink of the manuscript was drying, the first of the three existing original buildings of the early colonists in St. Mary's City was torn down for firewood. This was a little structure, medieval in appearance, the St. Barbara's barn, which had been owned by Mistress Mary Troughton, friend of Lord Baltimore, and which had later come into the possession of the Bromes.

Recently the second existing original building has had its face lifted. This is the Leigh House, which has been amputated by alterations inside and out, changing the place almost beyond recognition. Gone are the picturesque massive chimneys with little chimney pent, the carved stairway, and the kitchen-quarters building. Those who deplore these two pieces of destruction may find solace in knowing that the third original building in St. Mary's still stands well cared for and preserved: Clocker's Fancy.

Nevertheless, the Leigh House *was* the quaintest surviving early building in the first capital of Maryland, birthplace of religious freedom in this country. It would have been far easier and less costly to preserve the Leigh House than to rebuild and reconstruct it. Twenty years ago this writer called attention publicly to the "Fire, vandalism, panel-stripping, decay, neglect, and so-called improvements" which were sweeping the State of Maryland. In spite of widely-read warnings such as that, there are still those who "talk" about the restoration of St. Mary's City at the very moment, in this second half of the twentieth century, when the last vestiges of the town are disappearing.[3]

[3] For illustrations, see *Early Manors*, p. 202 (Kent Fort Manor), and *Jamestown and St. Mary's*, pp. 303 and 315 (Leigh House).

The Thomas O. Mathews Barn & House, Baltimore County

BIBLIOGRAPHY

Archives of Maryland, Baltimore, Md., 1883-1954.

Barney, H. C., The Green Rose of Furley, N.Y., 1953.

Bryant and Gay, Popular History of the United States, 1878.

First Annual Pilgrimage of Old Homes and Landmarks in Berlin, Worcester County, Maryland, Berlin, Md., 1953.

Forman, H. C., Early Manor and Plantation Houses of Maryland, Easton, Md., 1934.

Forman, H. C., Jamestown and St. Mary's, Baltimore, Md., 1938.

Forman, H. C., The Architecture of the Old South, Cambridge, Mass., 1948.

Forman, H. C., The Turner Family of "Hebron" and Betterton, Maryland, Baltimore, Md., 1933.

Henry, Mrs. R. G., Old Gardens of Talbot County, Maryland, Williamsburg, Va., 1947.

Kennedy, J. P., Rob of the Bowl, Philadelphia, 1838.

Lockwood, A. G., ed., Gardens of Colony and State, N.Y., 1931-4, 2 vols.

Maryland, American Guide Series (WPA), N.Y., 1940.

Maryland Historical Magazine, Baltimore, Md.

Ridgeley, H. W., The Old Brick Churches of Maryland, N.Y., 1894.

Skirven, P. G., The First Parishes of the Province of Maryland, Baltimore, Md., 1923.

St. Andrew's P. E. Church, Vestry Records, Maryland Historical Society, Baltimore, Md.

Tilghman, O., History of Talbot County, Maryland, Baltimore, Md., 1915, 2 vols.

Waterman, T. T., and Barrows, J. A., Domestic Colonial Architecture of Tidewater Virginia, N.Y., 1932.

William and Mary College Quarterly, Williamsburg, Va.

INDEX

Court House
1794

Young Men's Shop
formerly part
of Brick Hotel

Easton
National
Bank

Trader's
formerly
S.E.
Shannahon

McRory's

Read's
formerly
Kennard's
1801

Lomax

Fox Bros.
formerly
Chisolm

Maga-
zine
Alley

Bala
forme
Coving

THE OLD COURT HOUSE

A TENTATIVE RECONSTRUCTION BASED ON THE A